Richard Marsh is Canon Librarian of Canterbury Cathedral and was previously the Archbishop of Canterbury's Secretary for Ecumenical Affairs. He is a frequent traveller within the Oriental Orthodox world and is the editor of *Black Angels: The Art and Spirituality of Ethiopia* (Lion, 1998).

PRAYERS FROM THE EAST

Traditions of Eastern Christianity

Richard Marsh

First published in Great Britain in 2004 by
Society for Promoting Christian Knowledge
Holy Trinity Church
Marylebone Road
London NW1 4DU

British Library Cataloguing-in-Publication Data
A catalogue record for this book is available from the British Library

ISBN 0-281-05417-7

1 3 5 7 9 10 8 6 4 2

Typeset by Avocet Typeset, Chilton, Aylesbury, Bucks
Printed in Great Britain by Cromwell Press Ltd

In memory of His Holiness Garegin I,
Supreme Catholicos of All Armenians:
a friend and mentor

Contents

Acknowledgements	ix
Introduction	1
Armenian Prayer of Guidance	9
St Gregory the Illuminator	10
St Gregory of Narek	13
Hovhannes Garnetsi	16
St Mesrob Mashtots	17
Sabak Dzorop'orets'i	20
An Armenian Blessing	23
Armenian Prayer before Retiring at Night	24
Opening of the Armenian Orthodox Liturgy	25
Armenian Liturgy: Confession of the Clergy	27
Armenian Liturgy: Confession of the People	29
Armenian Liturgy: The Peace	31
Armenian Prayers of Intercession	33
Armenian Preparation for Distribution	35
Armenian Prayer before Meals	37
Armenian Prayer for All Occasions	38
Armenian Marriage Service	39
From Armenian Matins	42
From the Armenian Memorial Office	44
Coptic Anaphora of St Cyril	46
Coptic Beginning of the Anaphora	48
Coptic Blessings	50
Coptic Intercession	52
Coptic Kiss of Peace	54
Kiss of Peace from the Liturgy of St Cyril	56
Coptic Litany of the Congregation	57
Coptic Liturgy of St Cyril: Prayer of Reconciliation	59
Coptic Orthodox Compline	61
Coptic Orthodox Intercession of the Most Holy Mother of God	65

Coptic Orthodox Midnight Prayers 68
Coptic Orthodox Prayer before Communion 71
Coptic Orthodox Prayer after Communion 72
Coptic Orthodox Prayer before Meals 73
Coptic Orthodox Prayer for the Third Hour 74
Coptic Orthodox Prayer of the Veil 77
Coptic Orthodox Prime 79
Coptic Orthodox Vespers Prayers 81
Coptic Prayer for Laying On Hands 85
Coptic Prayer for Those Who Have Asked for Prayers 87
Coptic Prayer of St Severus 88
Coptic Orthodox Prayers before and after Confession 89
Ethiopian Anaphora of the Apostles 91
Ethiopian Prayer: Pilot of the Soul 93
Ethiopian Prayer to the Virgin 94
Indian Orthodox Prayers for the Morning 96
Syrian Beginning of the Liturgy of Our Lady 97
Syrian Anaphora of St James 99
Syrian Canon of the Faithful Brethren 103
Syrian Epiclesis: The Invocation of the Holy Spirit 104
Syrian Evening Prayer 106
Syrian Homily of St Jacob of Serugh 111
Syrian Hymn before Communion 113
Syrian Hymn of Mar Ephrem the Syrian for Compline 114
Syrian Introduction to Prayer 117
Syrian Introduction to the Lord's Prayer 119
Syriac Liturgical Supplications 121
Syriac Post-Communion Homily of St Jacob 124
Syriac Praise of the Cherubim 126
Syrian Prayer of Divine Dispensation 127
Syrian Prayer of Thanksgiving 129
Syrian Prayer of the Ninth Hour 131
Syrian Prayers of Confession and Absolution 132
Syrian Prayers for the Kiss of Peace 134
Syrian Prayers for the Morning 136
Syrian Prayers during Passiontide 140
Syrian Supplication to the Blessed Virgin 142
The Blessing of an Icon in the Syrian Tradition 144

Acknowledgements

I would like to thank my wife, Elizabeth Marsh, for all her help and encouragement at all stages of this project. I would also like to thank my editor, the redoubtable Ruth McCurry.

Introduction

Beginnings

When I went to work on the ecumenical staff of the Archbishop of Canterbury ten years ago now, the first thing to confront me was the filing system. It made up nearly a whole wall of the general office. For ease of identification, churches were colour coded – the Orthodox Churches were grey, the Lutheran and Reformed yellow and I forget now the colour of the Roman Catholic ones. But towards the beginning of this ancient and venerable filing collection was a run of orange files whose prefixes were AOC. I remember asking my equally ancient and venerable secretary what AOC stood for, only to be told, with a predictable look of disdain at my palpable ignorance, that it stood for Ancient and Oriental Churches.

I can recall withdrawing the files with a sense of great fascination. The files spoke of wondrous and romantic places with names heavy with resonance: Syria, Egypt, Armenia, Ethiopia, Eritrea and India. This was the stuff of dreams, but in my hands there was more than fantasy. For these were real places with living Christian traditions, but from an office in grey and wet London they seemed very exotic indeed.

In the course of the next few years I visited each one of these Ancient and Oriental Orthodox Churches in their homelands. I got to know their church leaders and their people. I got to know them as living entities with history, hopes and fears. I also got to know their communities in London and will always be profoundly grateful for their kindness and hospitality. The more I spent time working and praying with these churches the more I began to realize that they each had traditions of liturgy and prayer that were unique and particularly rich. The texts in

1

this book are chosen to reflect this and, hopefully, to reflect the delight which filled me as I got to know these traditions, which still can excite and illuminate.

What's in a name?

But I begin with a problem not of my own making, and it's the official term Ancient and Oriental Orthodox Churches or, more usually these days, Oriental Orthodox Churches. When I first came across it I was not sure that it worked as a term – and I am sure it doesn't work now. More importantly, I know that many members of the Churches covered by this cumbersome portmanteau find it both baffling and, sometimes, offensive.

And they have a point: describing something as 'Oriental' makes a presumption about who is doing the describing and from where are they doing it. Oriental Orthodox is a label bestowed by the Western Church, something which has conveniently stuck rather than something which really describes this family of Churches. Does it matter? It is not for me, a Western Christian, to make that sort of judgement. But there is a perfectly reasonable principle that out of respect you call people what they want to be called.

For the moment, I'm afraid that we'll have to stay with this description, acknowledging its inadequacy and passing on swiftly to naming and describing the Churches themselves.

A family resemblance?

The six Churches I have named are rooted in the tradition of Eastern Christianity. These are independent, national Churches, each with its own sorts of distinctiveness in traditions and praxis. But they are in communion with each other; that is, they have that intimacy of relationship whereby members of one of these Churches can share the Eucharist at the others' altars.

They are not in communion with the rest of the Orthodox Churches, for example the Russian Orthodox Church and the Church of Greece, which may be more familiar to Western Christians. This is because, historically, these Churches rejected

2

the definition of the person of Christ that was agreed at the Council of Chalcedon, a suburb of Constantinople, in 451. The Chalcedonian definition argues that Christ had two natures, human and divine, which were undivided and unconfused in his person. Those rejecting the definition erred on the side of the formula of St Cyril of Alexandria, who spoke of 'the one incarnate nature of the Word of God'.

Sometimes the Churches which rejected the Chalcedonian solution have been unfairly caricatured as *Monophysite*, that is, believing that Christ had only one nature. Today few would seriously accuse these Churches of heresy and it is agreed that differences, if any there be, are of a semantic nature rather than reflecting a real difference of opinion.

Armenian Apostolic Church

Modern Armenia is less than a third of the size of classical Armenia, and became independent at the break-up of the Soviet Union in the late 1980s. It lies in the north of the Transcaucasus between Turkey, Iran and Georgia, and is a country of mountains and great lakes and whose inhabitants grow remarkable apricots and distil fine brandy.

In 301, St Gregory the Illuminator converted King Tiridates of Armenia to Christianity, and Armenia became thereby the first country to adopt Christianity as its state religion. The centre of the Armenian Church has always been in Tiridates' capital, Etchmiadzin, where a cathedral is the spiritual heart of the Church. There were no Armenian bishops at the Council of Chalcedon, and it was only in 560 that a synod of the Church rejected the christological definition. In the eleventh century the ancient kingdom of Armenia was destroyed and a new one established in Cilicia in modern Turkey, from where Armenians had extensive contact with Frankish Crusaders. This kingdom too was destroyed in the fourteenth century. However, Armenian Christianity, with its distinctive language and cultural traditions, survived.

It survived, too, the genocide of the Armenians by the Turks in the late nineteenth and early twentieth centuries.

Some 1.5 million Armenians died in this genocide, and Armenians were dispersed even more widely across the globe. Today there are two Catholicossates and two Patriarchates, but the supreme Catholicossate is in Etchmiadzin. The Armenian liturgical traditions date mostly from the fifth to seventh centuries, with influences from Byzantium and later from the Latin West.

To join the Armenians for worship in their cathedral at Etchmiadzin is to enjoy a rich experience of devotion. The Armenian tradition of music is especially strong, and I find myself asking whether all Armenians sing so beautifully. The faithful are respectful and quietly devoted while priests (with their characteristic pointed hats) and choirs sing their devotions. And birds nesting in the vaults of the great cathedral join in their own songs of praise.

Coptic Orthodox Church

The Coptic Orthodox Church is the oldest Christian community in Egypt.

Founded, according to tradition, by St Mark, who died in Alexandria in 63, the Coptic Orthodox Church was originally a part of the Byzantine world. It is a Church that has always cherished its monasteries, which date from the earliest times. There are currently twelve monasteries, with a total of six hundred monks, and six convents, with a total of three hundred nuns. Monasteries have been particularly influential in the development of the life of prayer and liturgy.

The Church began to develop its own identity following its rejection of the Chalcedonian definition and its resistance to Byzantine efforts to enforce the definition. After the Arab invasion in 641, numbers steadily decreased, although Copts remain the largest Christian minority in the Middle East. I recall joining the monks of one desert monastery for vespers as night began to fall. There was a profound insistence about their careful chanting of the psalms. It was so dark in the monastery church that I could not make out faces of individuals but felt drawn into the community of prayer they had forged.

4

Leaving the monastery to drive back to Cairo, I saw the silhouette of a monk on the skyline, solitary, etched against the desert.

Syriac Orthodox Church of Antioch

Although based now in Syria, the Syriac Orthodox Christians are also to be found in Turkey and Iraq.

It is to the Christian community of Antioch recorded in the Acts of the Apostles that the Syriac Church traces its origin. Antioch was one of Christendom's great centres, but the definition of Chalcedon, although accepted in the urban areas, was never accepted in the rural areas. In the sixth century, the Bishop of Edessa, Jacob Baradai, ordained bishops and priests to carry on the non-Chalcedonian faith in the face of imperial opposition. Known sometimes as 'Jacobite' or 'West Syrian', it had its own liturgical tradition and maintained the use of Syriac as a vernacular language. Even today, in the Tur Abdin area of South East Turkey and in some villages in Syria, Syriac or Aramaic is still spoken.

Worshipping with the Syriac Orthodox is very special. Or rather, you feel that you are touching something very special because Syriac, the language of their worship, is essentially the Aramaic that Jesus would have spoken. I particularly remember a liturgy celebrated in the north-east Syrian town of Hassake near the border with both Iraq and Turkey, close to the heartland of Syriac Christianity.

The decline and eventual fall of Byzantium left the Syriacs free to engage in great missionary works as far east as China. Communities of spirituality and learning flourished in the Middle Ages. From Tamerlane's Mongol invasion until today, Syriac Christianity has declined under a constant stream of attrition. The decline of Syriac Christians or 'Suriani' in the Tur Abdin region has been particularly marked. Some monasteries remain in and around Mardin and there are three in the diaspora.

Malankara Orthodox Syrian Church

Syriac Christianity in south India traces itself right back to the apostle Thomas. By the mid-seventeenth century, most of these 'Thomas Christians' were concerned about the progressive latinization of their practices as a result of Roman Catholic Portuguese missions. In 1652, thousands of Thomas Christians refused to submit to Rome and petitioned the Syrian Patriarch of Antioch, who sent a bishop to offer pastoral care. In the twentieth century, splits and lawsuits within the community led to there being an autonomous Indian Malankara Church and a Church loyal to the Patriarch of the Syriac Orthodox Church in Damascus.

Worship is according to Syrian models but in the local language of Malayalam, a language that bubbles along at a great pace. There are elegant lofty churches often with ceiling fans to assuage the heat and great humidity of the Malabar coast of Kerala. This landscape is soft and well cultivated, especially with spices and exotics. Somehow this Church seems to fit into the landscape, and while not abandoning the Syriac models of worship, is authentically Indian.

Ethiopian Orthodox Tewahedo Church

Ethiopians are very proud of the tradition of the Ethiopian eunuch in the Acts of the Apostles, who was evangelized and baptized by the apostle Philip. They are equally proud of the tradition that the Queen of Sheba came from Axum in northern Ethiopia to see Solomon the Great. She left, pregnant, and her son Menelik returned to Jerusalem only to steal the Ark of the Covenant.

According to an ancient tradition, the first great evangelizer of the Ethiopians was St Frumentius, a Roman citizen from Tyre who had been shipwrecked along the African coast of the Red Sea. He gained the confidence of the emperor at Aksum and eventually brought about the conversion of his son, who later became Emperor Ezana. Ezana in turn introduced Christianity as the state religion around the year 330. Frumentius was ordained a bishop by St Athanasius of Alexandria and returned to Ethiopia to help with the continued evangelization of the country.

Around the year 480 the 'Nine Saints' arrived in Ethiopia and began missionary activities. According to tradition they were from Rome, Constantinople and Syria. They had left their countries because of their opposition to Chalcedonian Christology. The Nine Saints are credited with largely wiping out the remaining paganism in Ethiopia, with introducing the monastic tradition, and with making a substantial contribution to the development of Ge'ez religious literature by translating the Bible and religious works into that classical Ethiopian language. The very negative experience of contact with Portuguese Roman Catholic missionaries in the sixteenth century was followed by centuries of isolation from which the Ethiopian Church has only recently emerged.

This Church is unique in retaining several Jewish practices such as circumcision, and the observance of dietary laws and Saturday as well as Sunday sabbath. This is probably due to the fact that the earliest presence of Christianity in Ethiopia had come directly from Palestine through southern Arabia. But there is a tradition that Judaism was practised by some Ethiopians even before the arrival of Christianity. The Ethiopian liturgy is of Alexandrian (Coptic) origin and influenced by the Syriac tradition. The liturgy was always celebrated in the ancient Ge'ez language until very recent times. Today a translation of the liturgy into modern Amharic is being used increasingly in the parishes. A strong monastic tradition continues.

Worship with the Ethiopians is an experience of great intensity. Choir men beat huge drums with hypnotic rhythms and shake *sistra* or liturgical rattles. And they dance a long sinuous dance of praise. There is an extraordinary interplay of priests and people and stunning clothes of many colours. On important feast days thousands can gather at major churches and see the *tabots*, representations of the Ark of the Covenant, brought out in solemn procession. The Ethiopian Church offers a hint of what Christianity looked like in the medieval West: gaudy, abundant and deeply devoted.

Eritrean Orthodox Church

The Eritrean Orthodox Church was granted independence from the Ethiopian Orthodox Church in 1993. It has close links with the Coptic Church, from which it derives its episcopal lineage.

Concluding thoughts

Each of these Churches traces its origin back to apostolic times and persons, not in an antiquarian or abstract way, but as a guarantor of the authenticity of its articulation of the faith. The faith that they proclaim and explore now is that which was delivered to them in the beginning. But these are also very much communities for today. Many of them have suffered persecution and some continue to do so. Many are facing the huge challenges of modernity. But all represent a rich seam of Christian witness for which we should give thanks.

Armenian Prayer of Guidance

Guide us, O Lord our God,
and teach us to walk in thy paths of righteousness.
Keep our lives in peace, and our ways pleasing in thy
    sight.
Guide thy servants on their earthly and heavenly
    course
along thy paths of purity unto thine only-begotten
    Son,
our Lord and Saviour Jesus Christ,
who became our Prince of life and the hope of our
    salvation,
with whom thou art blessed, O Father Almighty,
together with thy life-giving and liberating Holy Spirit,
now and for ever, world without end. ✠ Amen.

Some prayers require little more commentary than to note that
they have an exquisite structure. This is one of them – a beautifully balanced prayer of simple devotion and elegant phrasing.

St Gregory the Illuminator

A prayer for times of trouble

Blessed is your love for mankind,
my Lord and Saviour Jesus Christ.
Why do you forsake me?
You alone are without sin,
and your name shows kindness and love for mankind.
Show me compassion, for you alone love mankind.
Save me, who have fallen into sin,
for you alone are without sin.
Remove me from the mire of my iniquity,
for I am submerged for ever and ever.
Save me from my enemies, for like a lion they growl
    and roar,
seeking to swallow me up.
Now, my Lord, flash your lightning
and destroy their power.
May they fear you and be cut off from the light of
    your face,
since they cannot stand in your presence, Lord,
nor in the presence of those who love you.
Whoever calls on you sees the power of the sign of
    your cross, Lord,
and trembles and shies away from it.
Now, Lord, save and keep me,
for I have put my trust in you.
Liberate me from my trouble,
so that the malicious one will not cast me into
    oblivion,
for he battles against me in his insidious ways.
Even over secrets you have dominion, Lord,
and you search the hearts and innermost being.
Purify my heart and my thoughts of all lewd and vile
    thoughts
so that I will not be lost into eternal perdition.
Have mercy on me, God, who have power over all,

and grant the grace of tears to my sinful soul,
so that I may wash away the multitude of my sins;
so that I may be saved from the hand of merciless
   angels
who cast innocent ones into the fires of hell.
I should weep continually, praying to you, God,
that I may not be found unworthy at that hour
when you will come, lest I hear that awful voice,
'Begone servant of evil. I do not know where you are
   from.'
Exalted God, the only sinless one,
grant me, this sinner, your abundant compassion on
   that day,
so that my secret wickedness will not be revealed
in the sight of the angels and archangels,
the prophets, the apostles and all the righteous.
But save me, this wicked one, by the grace of your
   mercy.
Receive me into paradise with the perfectly just.
Receive the prayers of this your sinful servant
by the intercession of the saints who are pleasing to
   you,
Jesus Christ, our Lord.
Glory to you with the Father and the Holy Spirit
unto the ages of ages. ✠ Amen.

Gregory is venerated as the founder of the Armenian Church
and his relics are greatly revered in the holy city of Etchmiadzin. This prayer of his reflects the tumultuous times in
which he lived, and, indeed, it could be argued that Armenians
have always lived in difficult and tumultuous times. Within the
last century 1.5 million Armenians were killed in the genocide
and millions more exiled from their native land so that there are
now many more Armenians living outside their native land than
in it. Armenians as a people have a remarkable and humbling
resilience, and the role of their faith in maintaining that is
significant.

In this prayer, Gregory draws on rich biblical imagery, which he adapts to his own purposes. There are allusions to Scripture, echoes that send the mind looking for connections. Yet Gregory has a strong and unique authorial voice. This is the prayer of a man of faith and authority.

St Gregory of Narek

A prayer of the Divine Liturgy to the Holy Spirit

Almighty, beneficent, loving God of all,
Creator of everything visible and invisible,
Saviour and Restorer, Provider and Pacifier,
O mighty Spirit of the Father,
we entreat you with open arms
and pray with sighs and cries,
standing before your awe-inspiring presence.
We draw near with great trembling and utmost fear
to offer first this reasonable sacrifice to your
    unsearchable power,
as to the sharer of the inalienable honour of the Father
in enthronement, in glory and in creation,
to you, the searcher of the hidden depth of the
    mysteries
of the all-perfect will of the Father of Emmanuel,
who sends you and who is the Saviour,
the giver of life and the Creator of all.
Through you, the three persons of the one God
were made known to us.
You too, O incomprehensible One,
are recognized as one among them.
With you and through you,
the early scions of the patriarchal family,
named seers, declare in plain language
the things past and the things to come,
the things that have been
and the things that have not yet come to be.
O Spirit of God, uncircumscribed power that you are,
by being proclaimed through Moses
to be the one moving on the surface of the waters
and brooding with tremendous envelopment,
and covering and defending the newly born
under your wings in tender love,
you made known the mystery of the baptismal font.

In the pattern of the archetype, before constructing
the pliable substance with its final covering,
you formed in lordly manner, O Mighty One,
the complete natures of all beings
and of all things, out of nothing.
Through you all your creatures are created
for the renewal of the resurrection,
which will be in that time
which is the last day of this life
and the first day of the land of the living.
The firstborn Son,
being of the same generation as you,
and of the same essence of the Father,
obeyed you also with oneness of will,
as he did his Father.
He, being in our likeness,
announced you to be the true God,
equal and consubstantial to his mighty Father.
He declared blasphemy against you to be unforgivable
and he stopped the impious mouths of them
that rebel against you, as of such as fight against God,
while he forgave blasphemy against himself,
the righteous and the spotless one, finder of all,
who was betrayed for our sins
and rose again for our justification.
Glory to him through you,
and praise to you with the Father Almighty,
unto the ages of ages. ✛ Amen.

Although used week on week in the liturgy, to our minds this
prayer may seem strange and almost impenetrable. Gregory of
Narek (951–1003) is regarded as the greatest figure in medieval
Armenian theology and literature. His greatest works are the 95
meditations in *The Book of Lamentations*, which is regarded as
having healing powers to the extent that it is sometimes placed
under the pillows of those who are sick.

The elegance of Gregory's Armenian resists easy translation

into English, where it ends up feeling theologically dense. It is an invocation to the Spirit at the beginning of the liturgy, a rehearsal almost of the whole of salvation history. There is beauty here, the beauty of forms and images in perfect balance. The believer reminds him- or herself of all that the Spirit is and all that it has done for them.

Hovhannes Garnetsi

A prayer for travelling

Leader to life, Path to truth,
our Lord Jesus Christ;
you led Joseph to Egypt,
and the people of Israel through the Red Sea;
and Moses to Mount Sinai,
and his people to the land of promise.
And you travelled with Cleopas and his companion to
    Emmaus.
Now, I pray you, Lord:
lead my companions and me
to travel in peace on the journey before us.
Save us from the visible and invisible enemy
and lead us safely to the place we are headed.
For you are our way and our truth and our life.
Glory and worship to you, now and always,
and unto the ages of ages. ✚ Amen.

Hovannes was born in Garni, a town not far from the modern
Armenian capital of Yerevan. He spent some of his early years
in the famously beautiful monastery of Geghard (c. 1180–
1245). He had great fame as an evangelist and travelled
fervently in Armenia and to the Holy Land.

This prayer reflects rather elegantly on journeys throughout
the Bible, summing them up in the journey made by Christ to
Emmaus. In this context, the journey that leads to the believer
embracing the mystery of the resurrection is the journey of us
all. In some respects this little prayer is a spiritual journey in
itself.

St Mesrob Mashtots

A hymnic prayer of reconciliation with God

Christ, God of gods, have mercy on me.

In iniquity did my mother give birth to me.
I beg you, Saviour, have mercy on me.
Wounded in sin, I fall down before you, Saviour.
Do not overlook me. Have mercy on me.

Sighing, the tax-collector received forgiveness in the
    Temple.
In his very words I too call out: 'Have mercy on me,
    God.'

The thief cried upon the cross: 'Remember me, Lord.'
In his very words I too call out: 'Have mercy on me,
    God.'

Pleading, the Prodigal Son begged you:
'Father, I have sinned against heaven and before you.'
In his very words I too call out: 'Have mercy on me,
    God.'

With the poor, Lord, grant us sobriety,
by the example of Lazarus, so that in voluntary
    poverty
we might be worthy with him of the Kingdom of
    heaven.
Hear us and have mercy on us, Christ God.

In place of the bread of deprivation,
you granted him the bread of immortality.
And contrary to the uncompassionate rich man,
you received Lazarus into the bosom of Abraham.
Hear us and have mercy on us, Christ God.

Enlighten the eyes of our heart so we may receive
the mercy that comes from you, Lord of mercy,
lest like the rich man in the fiery furnace,
we ask to be refreshed with a fingertip of water.
Hear us and have mercy on us, Christ God.

Together with the wakeful ones in heaven,
glorify the Almighty Father,
God who has no beginning!
With angelic voice, glorify
the only-begotten Son, begotten of the Father!
And with joyous sound, glorify
the Holy Spirit, the Restorer, with unceasing voice!
God without beginning and heavenly King,
glorified by the immortal heavenly hosts,
we bless you, O Father, without beginning.

You humbled yourself from the heights for our
     salvation,
O Liberator of bonds and Healer of our souls.
We praise you, O only-begotten Son.

Consubstantial with the Father
and glorified with the only-begotten,
distributor of gifts and bestower of mercy,
you we glorify, true Holy Spirit.

O Wisdom of the Father,
who shone the divine light of your Word
upon the darkness of ignorance enclosing the world,
enlighten us also.

You signified in the rich man and Lazarus
an example of the universal judgement
by handing them the contrary fates they received.

And so we shall ask you, Lord,
to save us from the fire of sin and suffering,
that we might rest in the bosom of the righteous
   patriarch.

With him, we too join the voice
of the choirs of angels singing
glory in the highest
to the indivisible Holy Trinity.

Mesrob Mashtots invented the Armenian script in or around 404 and in doing so laid the foundation of the rich literary tradition of the Armenian Church. He also composed many prayers still used on a regular basis in the Armenian Church.

This is a great example of the way that references to Scripture used cumulatively combine to give an extraordinarily rich picture of salvation. As our mind is taken in prayer from image to image, the believer is drawn into the heart of the mystery manifested in so many different ways. We begin with three examples of those who received forgiveness from Christ himself, after which the poet meditates on the story of Dives and Lazarus before associating his prayer with the sleepless host of heaven who are continually praising God.

This is energetic hymn-writing in which the niceties of doctrinal theology are never ignored, but drawn upon to enliven the spiritual life of the believer.

Sabak Dzorop'orets'i

A hymnic prayer for the Feast of the Holy Cross of Varak

By the sign of your all-conquering cross, loving Christ,
protect us against the invisible enemy.
For you alone are the king of glory, blessed for ever.

On this cross you spread out your undefiled arms,
and you poured out your blood for the salvation of
    the universe.
For you alone are the king of glory, blessed for ever.

When, at your second coming, this holy sign is
    revealed,
make us, your servants, worthy of the second renewal.
For you alone are the king of glory, blessed for ever.

May your cross be our refuge with its blazing
    brilliance.
That which is named the tree of life destroyed the
    enemy
and dissolved our death sentence, for the
    salvation of the universe.

Elevating it, heaven exults and the earth rejoices at the
    revelation
of the universal form of the four arms of the holy
    cross,
which illuminated the wood with rays like the sun.
Jerusalem exulted. The faithful rejoiced,
marvellously adorned, for they saw the triumphant
    sign.
All creation shone by its light.

You shone today the light of your unspeakable
  divinity
upon the cross, on the mount of Varak.
Blessed is the Lord God of our fathers!

You made known today the appearance of your
  awe-inspiring second coming,
by the sign of your cross, beaming it on earth.
Blessed is the Lord God of our fathers!

You gave a sign to those in fear, and a weapon against
  their enemy.
With it, protect those who believe in your holy
  Name.
Blessed is the Lord God of our fathers!

He adorned today the sign of the cross
with a heavenly light brighter than the sun.
Bless the Lord and exalt him for ever!

He revealed today the redemptive sign to the angels,
by descending to the mount of Varak.
Blessed is the Lord God of our fathers!

Come, all you saved by the life-giving cross,
bowing down to Christ our Saviour upon it.
Blessed is the Lord God of our fathers!

Another Catholicos, Sabak Dzorop'orets'i (c. 635–703), led
the Armenian Church through the cataclysm of the Arab inva-
sions in the late seventh century. The Armenians' turbulent
history of foreign domination drew them to contemplate with
particular devotion the mystery of the cross, by which Christ
transformed suffering and death into joy and life. This hymn

commemorates a miraculous apparition on Mount Varak in Armenia, and the discovery there of a relic of the true cross of Christ.

But it makes a wonderful commentary on the ornate crosses, or *khachkars*, that are found in so many Armenian churches. These are extraordinary feats of intricate carving where the cross has become a symbol of growth, binding foliage round itself. The cross – the place of death – is, in the Armenian tradition, a living place.

Throughout Armenia, but mostly in the environment of churches, you will find these remarkable monuments: crosses exuberant and almost organic in the richness of decoration and enthusiasm. This is the cross not as an instrument of torture, but of abundant life.

The Armenian Christian tradition, in common with most of the Oriental Orthodox Churches, does not have sophisticated theological traditions of icons as windows into the sacred. But these *khachkars* seem to serve something of that purpose. They take the worshipper to the heart of the mystery of Jesus' achievement in a subtle and almost tactile way.

An Armenian Blessing

Keep us in peace, O Christ our God,
under the protection of your holy and venerable cross;
save us from our enemies, visible and invisible;
and count us worthy to glorify you with thanksgiving,
with the Father and the Holy Spirit,
now and for ever, world without end.
✛ Amen.

This is a good example of a simple Armenian blessing of
dismissal – so good that it is even included in the Church of
England's *Common Worship*. But it gives a good example of an
important facet of Armenian spirituality, the devotion to the
cross, a devotion which is also expressed in the making of large
khachkars (see pp. 21–2).

Armenian Prayer before Retiring at Night

O Lord our God,
keep us in peace during this night and at all times.
Keep our hearts and thoughts secure in holy reverence
    for you,
so that we may be protected at all times from the snares
    of the enemy.
And let us offer blessing and glory
to the Father, and to the Son, and to the Holy Spirit,
now and for ever, and unto the ages of ages. ✚ Amen.

O Lord of hosts,
commit our souls to the angel of peace,
so that he may come and keep us in peace and
    undisturbed
by day and night, while awake and while asleep.
For you are the creator of light and establisher of night.
And now we ask you, Lord our God, grant us
to pass through this night's rest in peace and arrive at
    our morning duty,
to the worship and glorification of your All-holy Trinity,
now and for ever, and unto the ages of ages. ✚ Amen.

Night can easily be a time of uncertainty and fear, a time when malign forces are abroad and people can easily be tempted from the path of true faith and life. In prayers such as these we see the track-marks of a pre-modern world when night means a pathless and fearful darkness full of risk. The believer, preparing for night, places him- or herself into God's hands.

The knowledge that the mind and heart is as at risk as the body during the night hours is a psychological insight that has transcended the transition from the pre-modern to the modern world. Even today the passage of night with its 'fears and fantasies' can feel like a great journey, and we are wise to desire angelic assistance in order to bring us to morning and the worship of God.

Opening of the Armenian Orthodox Liturgy

Priest   I will give thanks unto thee with praises, O God my God.

Deacon   Then why art thou so heavy, O my soul, and why dost thou disquiet me? Put thy trust in God, give thanks unto him; the deliverer of my countenance is God.

Priest   Glory be to the Father, and to the Son, and to the Holy Spirit.

Deacon   Now and for ever, and unto the ages of ages. Amen. Again in peace let us beseech the Lord. Let us bless the Father of our Lord Jesus Christ, who hath made us worthy to come into this place of praise and to sing spiritual songs. Almighty Lord our God, save and have mercy.

Priest   In this dwelling of holiness and in this place of praise, in this habitation of angels and the house of mankind's expiation, before these symbols accepted by God and glorified, and before this sanctuary, we humble ourselves and bow down in fear, we bless and glorify thy holy, wondrous and triumphant dominion, and together with the heavenly hosts we offer blessings and glory unto thee with the Father and with the Holy Spirit, now and for ever, and unto the ages of ages. ✛ Amen.

All eucharistic liturgies in the Eastern Church do have beginnings, but often they are difficult to discern since they come after the end of matins and can be rather chaotic. These opening words begin with an expression of praise followed by

25

an almost apologetic and certainly poignantly hesitant expression of human diffidence in the face of the divine. Finally we find ourselves awestruck before holiness to which both the earthly and heavenly realms bear witness.

Armenian Liturgy: Confession of the Clergy

Deacon Let us make the holy Mother of God and all the saints intercessors with the Father in heaven, that he may be pleased to have mercy and compassion and save his creatures. Almighty Lord, our God, save us and have mercy.

Priest Receive, O Lord, our supplications by the intercession of the holy Mother of God, the immaculate birth-giver of thine only-begotten Son, and by the supplication of all the saints. Hear us, O Lord, and have mercy; forgive, expiate and remit us our sins; make us worthy to thank and glorify thee with the Son and with the Holy Spirit, now and for ever, and unto the ages of ages. ✠ Amen.

(turning to the congregation)
I confess before God and before the holy Mother of God and before you, fathers and brethren, and before you all the saints, all the sins that I have committed; for I have sinned in thought, word and deed and with all the sins that men commit. I have sinned, yea, I have sinned: I pray you, beg of God forgiveness for me.

Deacon May God Almighty have mercy upon thee and grant thee forgiveness of all thy transgressions of the past and present, and may he deliver thee from those of the time to come and may he confirm thee in all good works and give thee rest in the life to come. ✠ Amen.

The Armenian liturgy, in common with the Syriac, is celebrated on a raised staged area with a curtain known as a *bema*. But before ascending to celebrate the Eucharist, the priest begins standing among the rest of the faithful. There he prepares by confessing his own sins and asking for forgiveness. This is not theological and liturgical nicety, nor is it conceit or 'for show'. The integrity of any celebration of the Eucharist comes from the grace of God through the participation of the whole people of God. Standing among them the priest is fully a part of and yet representative of us all.

Armenian Liturgy: Confession of the People

Deacon With fear and with faith draw near and
communicate in holiness.

(Private prayer before confession)
O Lord, God of our salvation, who art merciful
and compassionate, long-suffering and full of pity
and repentance of the evil, yet I willingly gave way
to it and from good works I purposely kept away;
woe unto me *(3 times)*. I have sinned against God.

Priest May God grant thee forgiveness.

Deacon Reverend Father, I hold thee as reconciler and
intercessor with the only-begotten Son of God,
that by power given to thee, thou mayest release
me from the bond of my sins, I pray thee.

Priest *(Absolution)* May God the lover of man have
mercy upon thee, and grant thee forgiveness of all
thy sins, both those which thou hast confessed as
well as those which thou hast forgotten. Therefore,
with the priestly authority committed to me, and
by the divine command that whatsoever ye loose
on earth shall be loosed in heaven, I absolve thee
of all participation in sin, in thought, in word and
in deed, in the name of the Father, of the Son and
of the Holy Spirit, and reinstate thee in the
sacraments of the holy Church, that whatsoever
good thou mayest do, may be accounted to thee
for good and for the glory of the life to come. ✝
Amen.

(Private prayer after Holy Communion)
We give thee thanks, O Christ our God, who hast
granted us such a taste of thy goodness unto
holiness of life. Through it keep us holy and

without sin, by dwelling among us, and grant thy divine protection. Tend us in the pastures of thy holy and benevolent will, whereby, being fortified against every wile of the adversary, we may be counted worthy to hear thy voice, and to follow thee alone, our only victorious and true shepherd, and to receive from thee the peace prepared for us in thy Kingdom of heaven, O our God, and our Lord and Saviour Jesus Christ, who are blessed with the Father and the Holy Spirit, now and for ever, world without end. ✠ Amen.

Just before the moment of communion the worshippers have an opportunity to reflect upon and confess their sins, receiving God's forgiveness. In this life there is no more intimate encounter with Jesus than in the sacrament of his body and blood and it is somehow fitting that Christians should prepare themselves to receive this great gift. But the forgiveness of our sins is a gift in itself, freeing us from a great burden. In the absolution from the weight of our cares, and the reception of Christ in the Eucharist, we are refreshed and renewed.

Armenian Liturgy: The Peace

Priest   By the grace and everlasting kindness of our Lord
            and Saviour Jesus Christ, with whom unto thee, O
            Father, and also to the Holy Spirit, is fitting glory,
            dominion and honour, now and for ever, and unto
            the ages of ages. ✟ Amen. Peace unto all.

Choir   And with thy spirit.

Deacon   Let us bow down unto God.

Choir   Before thee, O Lord.

Deacon   Greet ye one another with a holy kiss. And ye that
            are not able to partake of this divine mystery
            begone without the doors and pray.

(The kiss of peace is passed throughout the congregation.)

Choir   *(Kiss of peace hymn)*
            Christ in our midst hath been revealed.
            He who is God is here seated.
            The voice of peace hath resounded.
            Holy greeting hath been enjoined.
            Here the Church is become one soul.
            This kiss is given for a bond of fullness.
            The enmity hath been removed.
            And love is spread over us all.
            Now ministers, raising your voice,
            give ye blessings with one accord
            to the consubstantial Godhead,
            to whom Seraphim give praises.

When Oriental Orthodox Christians think of the kiss of peace
within the Eucharist, they see themselves in direct continuity to
the Pauline injunction to 'greet one another with a holy kiss'. It

31

is a visible sign both of the unity of the community around the altar and the unity of that community with the whole Church of God.

When it comes to exchanging the peace, different Oriental Orthodox Churches have different practices that usually reflect the cultural norms and practices of the different societies. In the Armenian Church the person greeting says: 'Christ is revealed among us'; to which the reply is: 'Blessed is the revelation of Christ'. This is somewhat richer than the exchange we have in the Western Churches. At the peace in an Armenian church there is a sense of hubbub as the peace is exchanged while the choir sings a hymn with wonderfully sonorous harmonies.

Armenian Prayers of Intercession

Deacon   Of our leaders and first enlighteners, the holy apostles Thaddeus and Bartholomew, and of Gregory the Enlightener, of Aristakes, Verthanes, Yoosik, Gregoris, Nerses, Sahak, Daniel and Khad, of Mesrob the doctor, and of Gregory of Narek, Nerses of Kla, John of Orotni, Gregory and Moses of Tathev and of the Gregorians and the Nersesians and of all the pastors and chief pastors of Armenia, to be mindful in this holy sacrifice, we beseech the Lord.

Choir   Be mindful, Lord, and have mercy.

Deacon   Of the holy anchorites, the virtuous and God-instructed monks Paul, Anthony, Paulus, Macarius, Onophrius, the abbot Mark, Seraphion, Nilus, Arsenius, Evagrius, Barsumas, of the Johannesians, and of the Simeonians, and of the Oskians and of the Suckiasians and of all the holy fathers and of their disciples throughout the world, to be mindful in this holy sacrifice, we beseech the Lord.

Choir   Be mindful, Lord, and have mercy.

Deacon   Of the Christian kings, the saints Abgarius, Constantianus, Tiridates and of Theodosius and of all holy and pious kings and God-fearing princes, to be mindful in this holy sacrifice, we beseech the Lord.

Choir   Be mindful, Lord, and have mercy.

Deacon	Of all the faithful everywhere, of men and women, old and young and of every age, who in faith and holiness have fallen asleep in Christ, to be mindful in this holy sacrifice, we beseech the Lord.
Choir	Be mindful, Lord, and have mercy.

In common with many other Churches in the Eastern tradition, the Armenian Church reserves the part of the service just after the consecration of the bread and wine and the solemn invocation of the Holy Spirit as the appropriate point in the service for the prayers of the people.

The prayers begin with an account of the historic and foundational saints of the Armenian tradition together with historic rulers who have embraced Christianity, before moving to more contemporary rulers and the leaders of the Church.

Once again, the sense of the continuity of the Church in heaven and the Church on earth is made very strongly. The Eastern believer sees him- or herself as part of something much richer and greater than the merely here and now. We participate in the Church of the saints and they participate in our Eucharist.

Armenian Preparation for Distribution

Priest   Blessing and glory to the Father and to the Son
and to the Holy Spirit, now and for ever, and unto
the ages of ages. ✝ Amen.

Choir   The Father holy, the Son holy, the Spirit holy.
Blessing to the Father and to the Son and to the
Holy Spirit, now and for ever, and unto the ages of
ages. ✝ Amen.

Priest   In holiness let us taste of the holy and precious
body and blood of our Lord and Saviour Jesus
Christ, who, having come down from heaven, is
distributed among us. This is life, hope of
resurrection, propitiation and remission of sins.
Sing psalms unto the Lord our God, sing psalms
unto our heavenly King, the Immortal, who rideth
in cherubic chariots.

*(The curtain is drawn and the kneeling choir and deacons sing
'Lord, have mercy' alternately.)*

Choir   Lord, have mercy. *(4 times)*

Deacons   Lord, have mercy. *(4 times)*

Deacon   Upon the sick, bestow thy health; unto our
sleeping brethren, heaven. *Or:* Unto thy servants,
aid vouchsafe.

Choir   Lord, have mercy, Lord, have mercy, Jesus our
Saviour, Lord, have mercy.

Deacon   By the mediation of this holy and immortal
sacrifice.

Choir   Receive, Lord, and have mercy.

Private prayer after Holy Communion
We give thee thanks, O Christ our God,
who hast granted us such a taste of thy goodness unto
    holiness of life.
Through it keep us holy and without sin, by dwelling
    among us,
and grant thy divine protection.
Tend us in the pastures of thy holy and benevolent will,
whereby, being fortified against every wile of the
    adversary,
we may be counted worthy to hear thy voice,
and to follow thee alone, our only victorious and true
    shepherd,
and to receive from thee the peace prepared for us in thy
    Kingdom of heaven,
O our God, and our Lord and Saviour Jesus Christ,
who art blessed with the Father and the Holy Spirit,
now and for ever, world without end. ✚ Amen.

The use of medical language reminds us that metaphors of sickness and medicine have often been used to describe something of the activity of the reception of the Eucharist in the Western and Eastern Churches.

In the Armenian Church the communicant stands before the priest and says, 'I have sinned against God.' A particle of bread dipped in wine is then placed on the tongue. It is a moment often prepared for for many months.

Following the reception of communion and the singing of two hymns of praise and thanksgiving, the Last Gospel (John 1.1–18) is read. It is an interesting addition to the Armenian liturgy, coming from the Catholic Church via the Crusaders of the medieval period. Indeed, there are a number of liturgical practices (and indeed articles of clothing) which seem to owe their origins more to the West than to the East.

Armenian Prayer before Meals

The head of the table says:
O Christ our God,
bless this food and this drink of your servants with a
spiritual blessing, and make us healthy in soul and body;
so that as we enjoy the food our bodies require in the
modesty appropriate to our religious calling, we may
share in your infinite blessings, and in the Kingdom
of heaven, together with your saints. So that in
thanksgiving, we may glorify you, with the Father and
with the All-holy Spirit, now and always, and unto the
ages of ages. ✝ Amen.

All respond:
Let us eat this meal in peace, which the Lord has given
    us as a gift.
Blessed is the Lord for all his gifts. ✝ Amen.

Prayers of blessing before meals represent an intimate appreciation of the relationship between God and the Christian
community, and this is no exception. It is a simple prayer of
appreciation of God's gifts, a commitment to good sense and a
refusal of gluttony. But above all it is full of the appreciation
that no meal is eaten in isolation. All meals, no matter how
humble they may seem, are part of a greater banquet at which
Christ presides.

Armenian Prayer for All Occasions

Holy Saviour, Jesus Christ,
you are the true light that shone on the people of
    Armenia
through the preaching of St Gregory.
Remove from my life the darkness of despair, sadness
    and sin;
and replace them with the joy of your radiant love.
For you are the light of my salvation.
Blessing and glory to you, now and always, and for ever.
    Amen.

Armenia claims to be the world's oldest Christian nation. Tradition has it that the apostles Bartholomew and Thaddeus were the first to bring Christianity to the land that would later become Armenia.

But it is St Gregory the Illuminator, reputedly from Caesarea, who is looked to as the founder of Armenian Christianity as it has come down to us. He converted King Tiridates who in turn, in 302, proclaimed Armenia a Christian state. Gregory had a great vision of the descent of Christ and the establishment of the new Temple. The vision also included the watering of the land by many streams, and wolves attacking white lambs which are not defeated.

Tiridates renamed his capital city Etchmiadzin ('the only-begotten has descended'). Today it remains the spiritual capital of Armenia and the seat of the supreme Catholicos of All Armenians, or head of the Armenian Orthodox Church.

Armenian Marriage Service

Priest   O Christ our God, bless these wedding rings with
          a spiritual blessing, so that the people who wear
          them may not be approached by the wickedness
          of the evil one. Instead, may they be guarded and
          defended by the power of your holy cross, and
          may they be saved from all the snares of Satan.
          To you are due glory, dominion and honour, now
          and always and for evermore. ✝ Amen.

(The priest shall put the ring on the groom's left ring finger.)

Priest   O Lord, in your strength the King will be glad,
          and in your salvation how greatly he shall rejoice!
          You have given him his heart's desire, and you
          have not withheld the request of his lips.

Psalm 21.1–2

(The priest shall put the ring on the bride's left ring finger.)

Priest   The maiden will be led to the King in fine clothing;
          her virgin companions who follow her will be
          brought to you. They will be led with
          gladness and rejoicing; they will enter the King's
          palace.

Psalm 45.14–15

*(The priest shall join the right hands of the groom and the
bride.)*

Priest   God took Eve's hand and placed it in Adam's right
          hand.
             And Adam said: 'This is now bone of my bones,
          and flesh of my flesh; she shall be called Woman,
          because she was taken out of Man.' For this

reason a man shall leave his father and his mother, and be joined to his wife; and they shall become one flesh. *(Genesis 2.23–24)*

Therefore, what God has joined together, let man not separate. *(Matthew 19.6)*

Deacon   O Christ, look upon us and have mercy on us, for your compassion is plentiful.

Christ, you are a father to orphans and a righteous judge to widows, for your compassion is plentiful.

Christ, you are the crowner of saints, and you listen to us and to their prayers, for your compassion is plentiful.

Priest   Beloved children, by God's ordinance and according to the canons of the holy patriarchs, you have come to this holy church to be crowned and lawfully wedded in holy matrimony. May God keep you in mutual love and in one accord. May he make you live to a ripe old age, and make you worthy of the unfading heavenly crown.

But you should realize that this world has all kinds of troubles. There is sickness; there is poverty; and there are other afflictions and trials. We pray that God will keep you away from all such troubles. Nevertheless, it is God's commandment that you help one another until death.

The marriage service of any church or faith community gives us a fascinating glimpse of the presuppositions and cultural expectations of marriage. The Armenian wedding service is no exception to this rule, with its careful use of Scripture and tradition. The couple are married in church; in a real sense the Church is the unbroken chain of Christian believers down the centuries.

Blessing the rings so that they become tokens of the safety from evil that Christ offers in the Church is just one point on this continuum. Before the couple exchange promises, as the bride receives the ring, selections from Psalms and other parts of Scripture underpin the sense that on this, the day of their wedding, the couple are crowned King and Queen. And, as in other Eastern Churches, real crowns are held over the heads of the couple. And then the organic and intimate relationship of Adam and Eve is recalled before that relationship is put into the context of Christ in whom all marriages are made.

Of course, the real ministers of this sacrament are the couple themselves and the role of the priest is theologically subservient to this. There is some hearty good sense built into the fabric of these words. Bad times come in marriages and it is the task of the Church to hold the new household in their prayers.

From Armenian Matins

Choir and congregation 'In the beginning' the Word newly created the heaven of heavens out of nothing, and the celestial hosts: the watchers, the angels and the sensible elements contrary one to the other and yet agreeing, by which the ineffable Trinity is ever glorified.

The thrice-holy One, dominion and Godhead in one nature, the light uncreated that creates, commanded that there be created light, which he made to shine on the first Lord's day that was Sunday, by which the ineffable Trinity is ever glorified.

O thou love, in love didst thou humble thyself and wast incarnate for our salvation, in the same body that was crucified, and laid in the tomb of death, this day as God didst thou rise and by angels wast thou proclaimed; come ye that are saved, sing with the angel praises to him that is risen.

O sons of Zion, arise, awake, give the good news to the bride of light; thy groom is risen and hast conquered death by his power; he will come to crown thee with glory; go forth before him bedecked with adornments; sing a new song to him that is risen, to the fruit of life for them that are asleep.

This is a prayer for the end of Matins on a Sunday morning. Perhaps we would find it difficult to imagine using a prayer like this in Western Christian worship, but it is a good example of the sort of prayer which is common in the Oriental Orthodox Churches. It is profoundly dogmatic (in the best sense of the word), proceeding carefully and logically from an almost credal exposition of God's work in creation, first of the heavenly, celestial realm within the context of the Holy Trinity. It then moves on to celebrate the sensible world – once again worshipping in the context of the Trinity. From there it turns to Christ's saving action, allowing himself to be crucified for the needs of the world, and, in a nicely placed theological connection, links that and the resurrection with the angelic realm to which we were introduced in the first paragraph. Finally, using the metaphor of the Church as the bride of Christ there is the most wonderful celebration of the work of resurrection making good God's promises for the whole of creation.

From the Armenian Memorial Office

We, priests and people,
entreat thee, merciful and good Lord,
with those who have fallen asleep in faith:
receive us who have the same hope
into the heavenly city, Jerusalem,
in which the just are assembled,
to sing and glorify always the three persons of
    the Trinity.

In the supernal Jerusalem,
in the dwellings of the angels,
where Enoch and Elijah live in old age like doves,
worthily glorified in the Garden of Eden,
merciful Lord, have mercy on the souls
of those of us who have fallen asleep.

The Armenian Catholicossate of Cilicia is in a bustling outer suburb of Beirut. Close to popular beaches and smart shops, its courtyard with marble flagstones is an extraordinary haven of calm in the midst of the day-to-day trading of a great Middle Eastern city. The cathedral, built in the 1930s, is of classic Armenian style with high walls and a cone tower. Beside it is a small chapel, beautifully formed and proportioned. One evening I found myself there with an old Armenian woman dressed all in black. She was piously wrapped up in prayers and paid no attention to me. By the light of candles I could see that on four sides of the chapel there were glassed-in niches, but at first I could not see what they contained. When my eyes had accustomed themselves to the darkness I saw that each of them was filled with human skulls and bones. These were just some of the 1.5 million Armenians who died at the hands of both Turks and Russians between 1915 and 1922. These particular unfortunates had died in the Syrian desert; their remains were now a powerful symbol of an experience which was etched deep in the hearts of the Armenian people.

Each week, after they have met to celebrate the Eucharist, Armenian Christians conclude their prayers with a brief memorial office in the course of which they commend the souls of their forebears to the care of God. It is a powerful moment. The Eucharist has been celebrated as the central act of worship and devotion by the earthly church community, but before it disperses it faithfully reminds itself that the Church is not confined either by place or by what Newman called 'the busy beat of time'. The language of both Old and New Testaments combines to paint a picture of the Church triumphant in the heavenly Jerusalem. And if, for Armenian Christians, there is always the corporate memory of so many dead in the early part of the twentieth century and many others scattered around the world, there is hope too and a profound sense of trust in God the Holy Trinity.

Coptic Anaphora of St Cyril

Priest   It is meet and right, meet and right, meet and right, for it is truly meet and right, holy and fitting, and beneficial to our souls, bodies and spirits, O Eternal Master, Lord, God, the Father, the Pantocrator, that we at all times and in all places of your dominion praise you, sing to you, bless you and serve you; and that we worship you, give thanks to you, glorify you and confess to you night and day, with unceasing lips, an unsilenced heart and unending glories. You are he who created heaven and that which is in heaven, and earth and all that is therein: the seas, the rivers, the springs, the lakes, and all that is in them. You are he who created man according to your own image and likeness; and created everything in your wisdom – your true light, your only-begotten Son, our Lord, God and Saviour, and King of us all, Jesus Christ, through whom we give thanks, and offer unto you with him and the Holy Spirit, the holy consubstantial and indivisible Trinity this spiritual sacrifice and this bloodless service.

For great is your Name, O Lord, among all the nations, and in all places sweet incense and pure sacrifices are offered to your holy Name and upon this sacrifice and this oblation.

Deacon   You who are seated, stand.

Priest   For you are above every principality and authority, and above every power, every lordship and every name that is named, not only in this age, but also in the ages to come.

Deacon   Look towards the east.

46

Priest	You are the One before whom stand thousands of thousands and myriads of myriads of holy angels and archangels serving you. You are the One before whom stand your two choirs of exceedingly honourable living beings, having six wings and a multitude of eyes, the Seraphim and the Cherubim. With two wings they cover their faces, because of your divinity which none can gaze upon nor comprehend, and with two they cover their feet, and with the other two they fly.
For at all times all things hallow you. But with all them that hallow you, accept also, O Lord, our hallowing, as we praise you with them, saying:
Deacon	Let us attend.
People	Holy, holy, holy, Lord of Hosts. Heaven and earth are full of your holy glory.

The Liturgy of St Cyril is used occasionally during Lent but represents a very ancient tradition of Coptic liturgical writing. Whether it can really be ascribed to St Cyril of Alexandria is a matter for scholarly debate. St Cyril represents for the Coptic Church the touchstone of dogmatic orthodoxy.

The preface begins almost dramatically with a repetition of 'meet and right', and other repetitions later in the prayer are not redundant but move the 'action' on. We should marvel at the fluid movement from the concentration on God as creator in the first part into the celebration of the Cherubim with its close verbal association with Isaiah 6. And in the early section we are aware that elements from the historic creeds of the Church are used as an intimate part of the prayer. An Egyptian writer once spoke of a theologian as 'one who prays in truth'. In this prayer, this 'praying in truth' is extended to us all.

47

Coptic Beginning of the Anaphora

Worthy and just!
Now we are standing together with the heavenly choirs.
We praise our Lord with the seven choirs of the angels
    and with the two choirs of Cherubim and Seraphim.
We become as the tenth choir of the heavenly creatures.

You who have given to those on earth, the hymn of the
    Seraphim, count us with the heavenly hosts.
As we are counted with the heavenly hosts, we ought to
    stand with them looking to the east; to the throne of
    the Sun of Righteousness.

Worthy and right, worthy and right,
truly, indeed, you are worthy and right.
You, who are Master, Lord, God of truth,
being before the ages and reigning for ever,
you who dwell in the highest and look upon the lowly;
you who have created the heaven, the earth, the sea and
    all that is therein,
the Father of our Lord, God and Saviour Jesus Christ,
by whom you have created all things, seen and unseen;
who sits upon the throne.

You who are seated, stand.
Before you stand the angels,
the archangels, the principalities, the authorities,
the thrones, the dominions and the powers.

Look towards the east.
You are he around whom stand the Cherubim
    full of eyes, and the Seraphim with six wings
    praising continuously without ceasing, saying:

Holy, holy, holy, Lord of hosts;
heaven and earth are full of your holy glory.
Glory be to you, who is worshipped by all the holy
    powers.

In the West, we would term this extract the 'Preface to the Eucharistic Prayer', culminating in the Sanctus, or 'Holy, holy, holy'. The whole Eucharistic Prayer is termed the Anaphora. The community has gathered to listen to the story of redemption read from the Gospel. It has then professed its faith and prayed for the needs of the Church and the whole created order. After the kiss of peace and the offering of the gifts the community begins the Great Thanksgiving.

We should not be too wary of the language about angels, although it may be slightly unusual and perhaps a bit alien. The Churches of Eastern Orthodoxy have a strong conception of the role of the unseen powers of heaven. The Eucharist is not just about the here and now. We are connected across time to the actual events of the Passion, which we make present in the context of our worship. But there is not just this linear connection; there is a vertical one. The Eucharist is celebrated in the company of the whole host of heaven. The whole of the Church praises God in unison, and in preparation for celebrating the Eucharist earth and heaven are united in praise.

Coptic Blessings

May God have compassion upon us,
bless us, manifest his face upon us
and have mercy upon us.

Lord save your people,
bless your inheritance, pasture them
and raise them up for ever.

Exalt the horn of the Christians
through the power of the life-giving cross;
through the supplications and prayers
which our Lady, the Lady of us all,
the holy Mother of God, St Mary, makes for us;
and those of the three great holy luminaries:
Michael, Gabriel and Raphael;
the four incorporeal beasts, the twenty-four priests, all
    the heavenly ranks;
Saint John the Baptist, the hundred and forty-four
    thousand, our lords the fathers the apostles, the three
    holy youths, Saint Stephen;
the beholder-of-God St Mark the Evangelist, the holy
    apostle and martyr;
Saint George, Saint Theodore, Philopater Mercurius,
    Saint Abba Mina, and the whole choir of the martyrs;
our righteous father, the great Abba Anthony, the
    righteous Abba Paul, the three holy Abba Macarii,
    our father Abba John, our father Abba Bishoi, our
    father Abba Paul of Tammoh, our Roman fathers
    Maximus and Domitius, our father Abba Moses;
the forty-nine martyrs and the whole choir of the
    cross-bearers;
the just, the righteous, all the wise virgins, the angel of
    this blessed day;
the angel of this blessed sacrifice;
and the blessing of the holy Mother of God, first and
    last;

[*If it is a Sunday*:
and the blessing of the Lord's day of our Saviour.]

May their holy blessing, their grace,
their might, their favour, their love and their help
be with us all for ever. ✢ Amen.

Christ our God, King of peace, grant us your peace,
establish for us your peace, and forgive us our sins.
For yours is the power, the glory,
the blessing and the might, for ever. ✢ Amen.

A shorter version of this blessing may be substituted! But this is
a pretty comprehensive list of the foundational saints of the
Coptic Church. Coptic Christians feel close to their forebears in
the faith so it is not surprising that they should be included in
the final blessing of the people, the conclusion of the liturgy.

There is a careful and cumulative logic behind the prayer,
beginning with an opening invocation redolent of the Aaronic
blessing in the Book of Numbers and then moving through
some material from the Psalms to the life-giving centre of the
faith in the cross of Christ. From there it moves to an invocation of Mary's help, addressing her as Mother of God, the
theotokos or God-bearer, as defined in the Council of Ephesus.
From there we race through the archangels and the four beasts
of the visions of Ezekiel, via St John the Baptist and the
144,000 righteous who will be saved (according to the book of
Revelation), to the apostles, St Stephen the first martyr and then
St Mark, who is looked to as the founder of the Church in
Egypt.

A number of martyrs are then included before a celebration
of the founders of Egypt's monastic heritage, including St
Anthony the Great. Angels and holy virgins are swept up in the
company of those whose blessing is called, before returning to
Christ from whom all blessings flow.

Coptic Intercession

Priest   Pray for the air of heaven, the fruits of the earth,
the rising of the waters of the rivers,
the seeds, the herbs, and the plants of the field;
that Christ our God may bless them,
bring them to perfection in peace without harm,
and forgive us our sins.

People   Lord have mercy. Lord have mercy. Lord,
have mercy.

Priest   Raise them to their measure according to your
grace.
Give joy to the face of the earth.
May its furrows be abundantly watered
and its fruits be plentiful.
Prepare it for sowing and harvesting.
Manage our life as deemed fit.
Bless the crown of the year with your goodness,
for the sake of the poor of your people,
the widow, the orphan, the traveller, the stranger,
and for the sake of us all, who entreat you
and seek your holy name.
For the eyes of everyone wait upon you,
for you give them their food in due season.
Deal with us according to your goodness,
O you who give food to all flesh.

Fill our hearts with joy and gladness,
that we too, having sufficiency in everything
always,
may abound in every good deed.

People   Lord have mercy.

This is another prayer which seems to have sprung directly from the life of the worshippers. We can almost see the Nile in drought or spate. All the best intercession, which is a co-operation with God in his work of creation, has an acute sense of person or place. Intercession of this kind always has an intimate relationship with the moment of offertory. We may bring bread and wine to the altar but we also bring the real concerns, hopes and fears of the people of God. In Canterbury, we place prayer slips left by our visitors on the altar as we celebrate the Eucharist. There is a sense in which these are entrusted to our safekeeping, and, as a worshipping community, our task is to make them a part of our daily offering.

Canterbury is a very long way from Egypt in all sorts of ways but I am struck by the way that this intercession is close to Scripture and to life and all its concerns. The opening paragraphs reflect the needs and concerns of a predominately agricultural community, but with such an authenticity that we can imagine incorporating such petitions into our own prayers. And, finally, having shared our own needs and fears and those of our communities, we end in a petition of praise – the heart of all praying.

Coptic Kiss of Peace

Priest   According to your good will, O God, fill our hearts with your peace. Cleanse us from all blemish, all guile, all hypocrisy, all malice and the remembrance of evil which leads to death. And make us all worthy, O our Master, to greet one another with a holy kiss; that without falling into condemnation, we may partake of your immortal and heavenly gift, through Christ Jesus our Lord.

Through him the glory, the honour, the dominion and the adoration are due unto you, with him and the Holy Spirit the life-giver; who is in one essence with you; now and at all times, and unto the age of all ages.
✚ Amen.

Deacon   Greet one another with a holy kiss.
Lord have mercy. Lord have mercy. Lord have mercy.
Yes, Lord, who is Jesus Christ, the Son of God, hear us and have mercy upon us.
Attend.

In the Coptic Church each person in the church turns towards the people around him or her and greets them with the 'holy kiss'. This is done by touching the fingertips of the person next to you and returning your fingertips and the 'kiss' to your lips. It has a pleasing intimacy about it. The offering of a gesture of peace is common to the Church both East and West. Ways of exchanging it may vary, but for reasons more to do with cultural norms than with theological niceties.

In the Western Latin rites the peace is normally exchanged just before the distribution of communion, after the prayer of consecration. Eastern rites, almost universally, place the exchange of peace after the gathering, or *synaxis*, that is, the opening of worship up to the proclamation of the Gospel. In faithfulness to Christ's injunction to make peace among ourselves before bringing the gift to the altar (Matthew 5.23f.) we offer our gesture of peace before bringing our gifts to the holy table.

This introduction to the kiss of peace asks God to cleanse the community of its faults. It has a sense of repentance and is perhaps more honest as a basis for self-examination than the forms of words we have become used to in the West.

Kiss of Peace from the Liturgy of St Cyril

O Prince of life and King of ages,
God unto whom every knee bows, of those in heaven,
of those on earth, and of those under the earth;
to whom everything is subject and in the bond of
    servitude,
bowing their heads to the sceptre of thy Kingdom:
unto whom the armies of angels give glory,
together with the heavenly hosts, and all spiritual
    natures,
with an unsilenced voice that utters your divinity.
And as you have taken pleasure in us, the poor
    inhabitants
of the earth, that we should do service to you,
not because of the purity of our hands,
for we have not done good upon the earth;
but you are willing to grant us,
the unfortunate and unworthy, of your purity:
accept us unto you, O Good [God] and Lover of
    mankind,
as we approach your holy altar
according to the multitude of your mercies.
And make us worthy of the heavenly peace that
suits your divinity and is full of salvation,
that we may give it to one another in perfect love
and that we may greet one another with a holy kiss.

The Liturgy of St Cyril, another form of the Communion Service used occasionally in Lent, sets the penitence of the congregation in a rather more cosmic context. Our own frailty and failing is set alongside the faithfulness of the whole company of heaven. There is an attractive honesty in placing ourselves ultimately in God's hands. It is his peace and his salvation, and we must co-operate in that in a way which suits his purposes.

Coptic Litany of the Congregation

Priest   Again, let us pray to God Almighty, the Father of our Lord, God and Saviour Jesus Christ.

Deacon   We ask and entreat your goodness, O lover of mankind; remember, O Lord, our congregation. Pray for this holy Church and for our congregations.

People   Lord have mercy.

Priest   Grant that they may be for us without obstacle or hindrance, that we may hold them according to your holy and blessed will.

The worship of idols, utterly uproot from the world.

Houses of prayer, houses of purity, houses of blessing, grant them to us, O Lord, and to your servants who shall come after us for ever.

The worship of idols, utterly uproot from the world.

Satan and all his evil powers, trample and humiliate under our feet speedily.

All offences and their instigators, abolish.

May all dissension and corrupt heresies cease.

O Lord, as at all times, now also humiliate the enemies of your holy Church.

Strip their vanity, show them their weakness speedily.

Bring to naught their envy, their intrigues, their madness, their wickedness, and their slander which they commit against us;

O Lord, bring them all to no avail,

disperse their counsel, O God, who dispersed the counsel of Ahithophel.

Ahithophel appears in the Second Book of Samuel, inciting Absalom to rise up against King David. His presence at the end of this prayer, a prayer for those in the congregation, found in the middle of the intercessions for the Church and the world, takes us in to the heart of the Coptic mindset. The language is uncompromising but redolent of a lot of Coptic hyperbole. We, reading it from far off, need to recognize in it the sense of a Christian community under stress both from outside and from within. Heresies (false doctrine or, probably better, poor doctrinal choices), factiousness and wickedness are damaging the integrity of the Church. In some ways this language and these concerns take us to those formative early centuries of Christendom. We may not want to use the same sort of language about our own Christian communities, but perhaps reading these unrestrained and heartfelt prayers we might reflect a little on those ways in which our own gossiping, malignancy and petty intriguing damage the integrity of the Body of Christ.

Christ is the lover of humankind and it is to him that we go to ask for his presence in our lives and our homes.

Coptic Liturgy of St Cyril: Prayer of Reconciliation

O Creator of all that is made,
of that which is seen and of that which is not seen,
who cares for all things; for yours they are.

O Lover of Souls; I seek your compassion, O Lord,
    Almighty.
I, poor, despised, and unprofitable as I am among your
    servants,
now drawing near to your Holy of Holies,
and about to touch this holy and mysterious sacrament –
give me, O Lord, your Holy Spirit:
that fire immaterial and incomprehensible that devours
    all infirmity
and consumes wicked inventions.
Let it kill the earthly senses of the flesh;
let it restrain the wanderings of the mind that lead it
to imaginations full of pain and passion.
And as it is proper for priests,
let it make me rise above all mortal thoughts,
and grant me the sanctifying words to fulfil
this offering now laid on the altar, the mystery of
    mysteries,
in the fellowship and communion of your Christ.
To whom with you and the Holy Spirit, the giver of life,
and of one essence with you, belongs glory
now, and unto the ages of ages. ✛ Amen.

Elsewhere we will notice that the Coptic Orthodox Church 'dramatizes' the relationship between God and humanity in a particular way. Here is a good example of prayer that begins with God and a description of the fiery passion of the Holy Spirit, awesome and dangerous. But against this are put human passions and the inattentive meanderings of human attention which can fuel them. Here we may have some difficulties with the sort of language used to describe human sinfulness. We are learning not to equate human bodiliness with sinfulness in a sharp distinction of flesh and spirit. So we have to handle a prayer like this with a degree of wariness. That said, even for those living in the West in the twenty-first century, the sentiments of this prayer are worthy of consideration.

Coptic Orthodox Compline

Behold, I am about to stand before the just Judge, trembling and exceedingly afraid on account of my many sins, for a life spent in pleasures deserves condemnation. But repent, O my soul, while thou art dwelling on earth, for the dust in the grave offers no praise; and the dead remember not, nor do they who are in Hades offer thanks. But arise from the slumber of indolence, imploring the Saviour and repenting and crying out, saying: 'O God, have mercy on me and save me.'

Glory be to the Father, and to the Son, and to the Holy Spirit.

If this life were permanent and this world eternal, thou wouldst have had, O my soul, an apparent excuse; but when thy bad deeds and shameful sins are exposed before the just Judge, what wilt thou give in answer while thou art lying down on the bed of transgression, slow to control thy body? O Christ, our God, before thy dreadful judgement seat am I afraid, and the counsel of thy judgement do I dread, and at the radiance of thy divinity do I tremble, I the wicked and defiled, who am lying down upon my bed, careless about my life. Yet like the publican, I beat upon my breast and cry: 'O God, be merciful to me, a sinner.'

Both now and ever, and unto the ages of ages. ✠ Amen.

O pure Virgin, draw the veil of thy speedy protection upon thy servant. Remove from me the billows of evil thoughts and raise my sick soul to pray and watch, because it has long lain in deep sleep; for thou art able, merciful, helpful and the birth-giver of the spring of life, my King and my God, Jesus Christ, my hope.

Grant, O Lord, that we may be kept this night without sin;

blessed art thou, O Lord, God of our fathers, and full of
blessings,
and glorified is thy holy name for ever. ✝ Amen.

Let thy mercy be upon us, as we have set our hope on
thee,
for the eyes of all hope on thee,
for thou givest them their food in due season.
Hear us, O God, our Saviour, the hope of all the earth,
and thou, O Lord, wilt keep us and deliver us from this
generation, and for ever. ✝ Amen.

Blessed art thou, O Lord, teach me thy righteousness;
blessed are thou, O Lord, make me understand thy truth;
blessed art thou, O Lord, enlighten me in thy
righteousness.
O Lord, thy mercy is for ever, despise not the works of
thy hands,
for thou, O Lord, art our refuge, from generation to
generation.
I cried unto the Lord and said:
'Have mercy on me and save my soul,
for I have sinned against Thee.'
O Lord, unto thee I flee for refuge,
save me and teach me to do thy will, for thou art my
God;
with thee is the fountain of life, and in thy light shall we
see light.
Let thy mercy come upon those who know thee,
and thy righteousness to the upright in heart.
Unto thee is due blessing, unto thee is due praise,
unto thee is due glory, O Father, Son and Holy Spirit,
ever existent. ✝ Amen.

Good it is to praise the Lord,
and to give thanks to thy name, O Most High,
to declare thy mercies in the mornings and thy truth at
every eventide.

The Trisagion

Holy God, Holy and Mighty, Holy and Immortal,
who wast born of the Virgin,
have mercy on us.
Holy God, Holy and Mighty, Holy and Immortal,
who wast crucified for us,
have mercy on us.
Holy God, Holy and Mighty, Holy and Immortal,
who rose from the dead and ascended into heaven,
have mercy on us.

Glory be to the Father, and to the Son, and to the Holy
  Spirit,
both now and ever, and unto the ages of ages. ✠ Amen.

O holy Trinity, have mercy on us.
O holy Trinity, have mercy on us.
O holy Trinity, have mercy on us.
Lord, forgive our sins, Lord, forgive our iniquities, Lord,
  forgive our trespasses.
Lord, visit the sick among thy people, heal them for the
  sake of thy holy name.
To the souls of our fathers and brothers who have fallen
  asleep, give repose.
O thou who alone art without sin, help us and accept
  our prayers.
For thine is the glory, dominion and triple holiness;
Lord have mercy, Lord have mercy, Lord send thy
  blessings. ✠ Amen.

The selections from the Book of Hours of the Orthodox
Church are primarily the prayer of monasteries and, conse-
quently, the prayer of the desert. Coptic Christians might well
use parts of these services in a domestic setting but essentially
they are the corporate worship of a monastic community gathering to mark the passage of the day in prayer. Traditionally,

63

Coptic monks spend most of their time alone in their cells, only coming together for worship. There are elements here which are familiar to those who use a Western form of Compline, but the relationship between God and humanity is prayed in a more dramatic way.

The desert intensifies the play of light. The inhabitants of desert places are particularly aware of the slightest changes in light, and this is reflected in their prayers. As the dark hours of night come upon them, the worshipper reflects on the consequences of being judged. The time for repentance is now, for there is no confession in the dust of the grave. The tone of the language feels different from some other examples from the Coptic corpus. There is a personal intensity here – the Christian standing before their judging God. Sometimes the language is admonitory, reflective. When Christ is first addressed, it is nervously, almost painfully. The image of the publican, honest in his humility, is a source of strength, and confidence builds as the worshipper places him- or herself into the loving judgement of God who cleanses and heals.

The Trisagion (Holy God, Holy and Mighty, Holy and Immortal, have mercy on us) is a prayer that is familiar in the worship of all Orthodox Christianity, both Chalcedonian and non-Chalcedonian. In this instance, there are confessional augmentations ('who was born of the Virgin' etc.) which enrich and strengthen its use in this context of death, judgement and submission.

Coptic Orthodox Intercession of the Most Holy Mother of God

Hail to thee.
We ask thee, O saint, full of glory, the ever-virgin,
the birth-giver of God, the Mother of Christ;
to lift up our prayers to thy beloved Son
that he may forgive our sins.

Hail to her, the saint, the Virgin,
who gave birth to the True Light, Christ our Lord;
may she ask the Lord to have mercy on us and forgive
    our sins.
O Virgin Mary, birth-giver of God,
the faithful intercessor of the human race,
intercede for us before Christ to whom thou gavest birth,
that he may grant us forgiveness of our sins.

Hail to thee, O Virgin, the true queen.
Hail to her who is the pride of our race,
who gave birth to Emmanuel.
We ask thee to remember us, O faithful intercessor,
before our Lord, Jesus Christ, that he may forgive our
    sins.

Introduction to the creed

We magnify thee, O Mother of the True Light,
and we glorify thee, O virgin saint, birth-giver of God,
for thou hast borne unto us the Saviour of the world;
he came and saved our souls.

Glory be to thee, O Christ, our Master and our King,
the honour of the apostles, the crown of the martyrs,
the rejoicing of the righteous, the confirmation of the
    Churches,
the forgiveness of sins.
We proclaim the Holy Trinity, one in essence.

We worship him and glorify him.
Lord have mercy, Lord have mercy,
Lord send thy blessings. ✝ Amen.

The creed

We believe in one God,
God the Father, the ruler of all,
who created the heaven and the earth,
and all things seen and unseen.
We believe in one Lord Jesus Christ,
the only-begotten Son of God,
begotten of the Father before all ages.
Light of light; true God of true God, begotten, not
created;
of one essence with the Father, by whom all things were
created.
Who, for us men and for our salvation,
came down from the heaven and was incarnate of the
Holy Spirit
and the Virgin Mary, and became man.
And he was crucified for us under Pontius Pilate,
suffered, and was buried.
And the third day he rose from the dead, according to
the Scriptures;
and ascended into heaven, and sits at the right hand of
his Father.
And he shall come again with glory to judge the living
and the dead,
whose Kingdom shall have no end.
And we believe in the Holy Spirit, the Lord, the giver of
life,
who proceeds from the Father;
who with the Father and the Son is worshipped and
glorified,
who spoke by the prophets in one Holy Catholic and
Apostolic Church.
We confess one baptism for the remission of sins.

We look for the resurrection of the dead,
and the life of the world to come. ✢ Amen.

These prayers form a part of the Coptic Orthodox liturgy of the
Eucharist. The Copts have a particular devotion to the Holy
Family, believing that it was to Egypt that Mary and Joseph fled
with the infant Jesus. This sense of Coptic Christians inhabiting
the same space as the Holy Family adds a special sense of intimacy and of place to Coptic spirituality.

Mary has a special place in the hearts of Coptic Christians
but no more so than for other Oriental Orthodox faith communities. These prayers, as with the best of all devotion to Mary,
focus not on her but on Christ. She points to him in his incarnate fullness. With her we acknowledge our weakness and pray
for forgiveness.

Coptic Orthodox Midnight Prayers

Behold, the Bridegroom comes at midnight. Blessed is that servant whom he shall find watching, but he whom he shall find sleeping is unworthy to go with him. See, O my soul, that you grow not heavy with sleep, lest you be cast outside the Kingdom, but watch and cry aloud, saying: 'Holy, holy, holy are you, O God!' For the sake of the birth-giver of God, have mercy upon us.

Glory be to the Father, and to the Son, and to the Holy Spirit.

O my soul, consider that terrible day, and awake and light your lamp with the oil of gladness, because you know not the hour when that cry comes upon you saying: 'Behold the Bridegroom is coming.' See, O my soul, that you sleep not, lest you be found outside, knocking like the five foolish virgins, but watch, that you may meet the Lord Christ with the oil of fatness and that he may grant you the true wedding of his divine glory.

Both now and ever, and unto the ages of ages. ✟ Amen.

You are a rampart of our salvation, O Virgin, birth-giver of God, and an invincible bulwark. Bring to nought the counsels of our adversaries, and the affliction of your servants turn into joy. Defend our city, fight for our kings, and intercede for the peace of the world, for you are our hope, O birth-giver of God.

Both now and ever, and unto the ages of ages. ✟ Amen.

O heavenly King, the Comforter, the Spirit of Truth, who are everywhere present, and fill all things, O treasury of good, and bestower of life, come and dwell in us, and cleanse us from every stain, and save, O Good One, our souls.

Glory be to the Father, and to the Son, and to the Holy Spirit.

As you were with your disciples, O Saviour, and gave them peace, come also and be with us, and save us, and deliver our souls.

Both now and ever, and unto the ages of ages. ✢ Amen.

When we stand in your holy temple, we are counted as those standing in heaven. You are the gate of heaven, O birth-giver of God; open to us the door of mercy.

O Lord, hear us, have mercy on us, and forgive our sins. Lord have mercy (Kyrie eleison).

Holy, holy, holy, O Lord of Sabaoth,
heaven and earth are full of your glory and your majesty.
Have mercy on us, O God, the Father Almighty.
O holy Trinity, have mercy on us.
O Lord of hosts, be with us,
for we have no other helper in our tribulations and
    necessities but you.
Loose, remit and pardon, O God,
our transgressions that we have committed
voluntarily and involuntarily,
consciously and unconsciously,
secretly and openly.
O Lord, remit them for the sake of your holy Name,
by which we are called,
according to your mercy, O Lord,
and not according to our sins.

Perhaps we have to imagine ourselves in a monastery out in the desert with the monks gathering together for their prayer at midnight. The quality of the spirituality of the desert is special and this has long been a significant underpinning for

Coptic Christianity. It is a Christianity forged in the crucible of the desert where emptiness heightens the sense of God's presence.

There is a feeling of urgency and the imminence of the end-times in these midnight prayers. They are a meditation based on Jesus' parable of the wise and foolish virgins. Jesus is the Bridegroom and the Church is called upon to be watchful and ready for his coming.

Coptic Orthodox Prayer before Communion

O Lord, I am not worthy that thou shouldest come
under the roof of my house, for I am sinful, but say thou
first a word and my soul shall be healed. Say unto my
soul: 'Thy sins are forgiven.'

I am barren and wanting all righteousness, and have
but thy compassion, mercy and love of man.

Thou hast condescended from the heaven of thine
ineffable glory to our afflictions and accepted to be born
in a manger. Refuse not, O my blessed Saviour, to come
into my lowly and afflicted soul that awaiteth thy
radiant presence. But accept to come into my soul to
cleanse it. O thou, who disdainedst not to enter into the
leper's house and to heal him, forbid me not to approach
thy pure Body and thy holy Blood.

O thou who preventedst not the woman who was a
sinner from kissing thy feet, let my communion be for
partaking with thee and for effacing all defilement, the
mortification of my lusts, the doing of thy life-giving
commandments, the healing of my soul and body from
all sins, the acceptance of thy gifts, the indwelling of thy
grace, the descent of thy Spirit for union with and
abiding in thee, that I may live for the glory of thy holy
Name. ✟ Amen.

The beginning of the prayer before communion will be familiar
to many Christians from its inclusion in Western liturgies. It
derives from Jesus' healing of the centurion's servant in chapter
8 of Matthew's Gospel. But the sense of humility, of being
unworthy for Christ (or the Eucharist) to enter is explored
further as the one praying recalls that God condescended to be
born in a stable. The prayer explores God's humility in Christ
as a way of developing thoughts about our own preparedness
to receive Christ in the Eucharist.

Coptic Orthodox Prayer after Communion

My heart has been filled with joy and my tongue with
rejoicing. Let my spirit glorify the Lord, and my soul
rejoice in God my Saviour.

I have drawn nigh to thee, O Lord, to clothe me with
a radiant garment and make me worthy to enter into thy
wedding.

Let my union with thee today be for ever, for through
it I increase and grow firm in virtue, wax strong in faith,
and strengthen my hope.

Let it become a sign of salvation, a raiment of grace, a
garment of the new birth, a purity and righteousness of
body and soul, a cleansing of love, an eternal happiness
and joy, a good answer before thy dreadful tribune.

I commit myself to thy compassion,
to make me one with thee and under thy will.
I call forth my mind and my senses to thee.
My will do thou bless to obey thy will.
Enliven my heart and awaken my conscience.
Disperse the fantasies of the adversaries.
Still the tempest. Walk with me and calm my terror.
Quench my thirst, kindle the flame of thy love in my
    heart.
Abide with me, for the day is far spent,
and accompany me until daybreak.
For thou art my goal and my happiness.
Thou alone, O Lord, for ever. ✠ Amen.

The post-communion prayer is an energetic affirmation of the
gift of the Eucharist. The language reflects the Magnificat and
other songs of praise. But even this prayer has a nervousness
about it. Despite the gift of God in the bread and wine there are
still human fears and forebodings with which to contend.

Coptic Orthodox Prayer before Meals

Blessed art thou, O Lord, who hast supported us from
our youth and granted unto us thy blessings, and
prepared food for every creature; for the eyes of all await
thee, thou who givest them their food in due season.
Thou openest thine hands and fillest all living things.

To thee is due glory, praise, blessing and thanksgiving
for the food that thou hast prepared for us.

Stretch forth thy right hand and bless this food set
before us for the nourishment of our bodies. Let it be for
power and health of our lives. Grant salvation, grace,
blessing and purity to all those who partake thereof.

Lift our minds to thee at all times to seek our spiritual
and eternal food. Grant that we may labour for the
everlasting food which is for life eternal. Grant us to be
partakers of thy evening banquet.

Grant us the food of blessing, the cup of salvation,
and fill our hearts with joy. Grant us a peaceful life, joy
of the soul and health of the body. Teach us to seek thy
pleasure in all things so that when eating, drinking or
labouring, we do it all for the glory of thy holy Name.
For thine is the glory, for ever and ever. ✠ Amen.

Though perhaps not the most economical of prayers, this grace
gets everything in the right relationship. God is blessed for
blessing us with the gift of sustenance and not just sustenance
for the body: the soul, too, is included. Everything is seen in the
context of the eternal and the glory of God.

All too frequently we lose a sense of the importance of food
and table fellowship in our fast-food world. Not so Christians
of the East, for whom food is valuable and precious, often hard
won from difficult landscapes. And fellowship at the table is
something to be carefully cherished and offered to God.

Coptic Orthodox Prayer for the Third Hour

Thy Holy Spirit, O Lord, which thou sent forth upon thy
    holy disciples,
and thine honourable apostles at the third hour;
this Spirit take not away from us, O Good One, but
    renew him within us.
Create in me a clean heart, O God, and renew a right
    spirit within me.
Cast me not away from thy presence, and take not thy
    Holy Spirit from me.

Glory be to the Father, and to the Son, and to the Holy
    Spirit.

O Lord, who at the third hour didst send down thy Holy
    Spirit
upon thy holy disciples and honourable apostles;
this Spirit take not away from us, O Good One,
but renew him within us, we beseech thee,
O Christ, our Lord and Word and Son of God,
a righteous and life-giving Spirit,
a Spirit of prophecy and purity;
a Spirit of sanctification, righteousness and power, O
    Almighty One.
For thou art the light of our souls,
O thou who enlightenest every man that cometh into the
    world,
thou who hast mercy on us.

Both now and ever, and unto the ages of ages. ✟ Amen.

Birth-giver of God, thou art the True Vine, bearing the
    Fruit of Life,
we ask thee, O thou full of grace, together with the
    apostles,
for the salvation of our souls.

Blessed be the Lord our God. Blessed be the Lord day by day.
The God of our salvation shall prosper us along the way.

Both now and ever, and unto the ages of ages. ✠ Amen.

O heavenly King, the Comforter, the Spirit of Truth,
who art everywhere present, and fillest all things,
O treasury of good, and bestower of life,
come and dwell in us, and cleanse us from every stain,
and save, O Good One, our souls.

Glory be to the Father, and to the Son, and to the Holy
Spirit.

As thou wast with thy disciples, O Saviour, and gavest
them peace,
come also and be with us, and save us, and deliver our
souls.

Both now and ever, and unto the ages of ages. ✠ Amen.

When we stand in thy holy temple,
we are counted as those standing in heaven.
Thou art the gate of heaven, O birth-giver of God,
open unto us the door of mercy.
O Lord, hear us, have mercy on us, and forgive our sins.
Lord have mercy (Kyrie eleison).

Holy, holy, holy, O Lord of Sabaoth,
heaven and earth are full of thy glory and thy majesty.
Have mercy on us, O God the Father Almighty.
O Holy Trinity, have mercy on us.
O Lord of hosts, be thou with us,
for we have no other helper in our tribulations and
necessities but thee.
Loose, remit and pardon, O God,
our transgressions that we have committed

75

voluntarily and involuntarily,
consciously and unconsciously,
secretly and openly.
O Lord, remit them for the sake of thy holy Name,
by which we are called,
according to thy mercy, O Lord,
and not according to our sins.

These prayers for midday focus on the gift of the Holy Spirit, and the worshipper prays to be strengthened by the Spirit. The office concentrates its meditative attention on Pentecost. Once again, the careful assembly of biblical texts, familiar and unfamiliar, gives a rich set of metaphors upon which to reflect. Here are metaphors which draw the worshipper deep into the mystery of God and paint a picture of the activity of the Holy Spirit, enlightening and sustaining the people of God.

Coptic Orthodox Prayer of the Veil

The Prayer of Thanksgiving

Let us give thanks unto the beneficent and merciful God,
the Father of our Lord, God and Saviour, Jesus Christ.
For he hath shielded us, rescued us, kept us,
accepted us unto himself, had compassion on us,
   supported us,
and brought us unto this hour.
Let us ask him also to keep us this holy day
and all the days of our life in all peace,
the Almighty Lord our God.

O Master, Lord, God Almighty,
Father of our Lord, God and Saviour,
Jesus Christ; we thank thee.
For thou hast shielded us, rescued us, kept us,
accepted us unto thyself, had compassion on us,
   supported us,
and brought us unto this hour.
Therefore we ask and entreat thy goodness, O lover of
   man,
grant us to complete this holy day,
and all the days of our life in all peace in thy fear.

All envy, all temptation, all the influence of Satan,
the intrigue of wicked people, the rising up of enemies,
hidden and manifest, take away from us,
and from all thy people, and from this, thy holy place.
But as for those things which are good and useful,
provide us with them. For thou art the One
who gave us the authority to trample
on serpents and scorpions and every power of the enemy.
And lead us not into temptation, but deliver us from the
   evil one,

through the grace, compassion and love of man,
of thine only-begotten Son,
our Lord, God and Saviour, Jesus Christ.

Through whom glory, honour, dominion and worship
befit thee with him and the Holy Spirit, the life-giver
who is of one essence with thee,
both now and ever, and unto the ages of ages. ✝ Amen.

Used both in the Offices and in the Eucharist, this is a Coptic
General Thanksgiving. It is a prayer of total submission to and
reliance upon God. At times it is repetitive but none the worse
for that. It is the prayer of those who know their need of God
and can recognize the activity of grace in their lives.

Coptic Orthodox Prime

O thou, the true light that enlightenest every man that cometh into the world, thou hast come into the world through thy love for mankind. All creation hath rejoiced for thy coming. Thou hast saved our forefather Adam from the beguiling and delivered our foremother Eve from the pangs of death. Thou hast given us the spirit of adoption; we praise thee, we bless thee, saying:

Glory be to the Father, and to the Son, and to the Holy Spirit.

When the morning watch dawns upon us, O Christ our God, the true light, let the enlightened senses and thoughts shine within us and let not the darkness of pains overcome us, that we may praise thee reasonably with David, saying: 'Mine eyes have awakened before the morning watch, that I may meditate on thy sayings.' Hear our cries according to thy great mercy, and save us, O Lord our God, through thy loving kindness.

Both now and ever, and unto the ages of ages. ✝ Amen.

Thou art the all-honoured Mother of Light. From the rising of the sun to the going down of the same, they offer thee praise, O birth-giver of God, for thou art the pure and unchanged blossom and the ever-virgin Mother, for the Father chose thee, and the Holy Spirit overshadowed thee, and the Son took flesh from thee. Ask him to grant salvation to the world which he hath created, and deliver it from temptation.
Let us praise him with a new song and bless him.

Both now and ever, and unto the ages of ages. ✝ Amen.

Let us sing with the angels saying:
'Glory be to God in the highest, on earth peace, goodwill
    towards men.'

We praise thee; we bless thee; we serve thee; we worship
thee;
we confess thee; we proclaim thy glory.
We thank thee for thy great glory.
O Lord, heavenly King, God the Father Almighty,
O Lord, the only-begotten Son Jesus Christ, and the
Holy Spirit;
O Lord, God, Lamb of God, Son of the Father,
who takest away the sins of the world, have mercy on
us.
O thou, who takest away the sins of the world, accept
our prayers.
O thou, who sittest at the right hand of thy Father, have
mercy on us.
Thou alone art holy; thou alone art the most high,
my Lord Jesus Christ and the Holy Spirit.
Glory be to God the Father. ☩ Amen.

Every day I will bless thee, and praise thy holy Name for
ever,
and unto the ages of ages. ☩ Amen.

From the night, my spirit seeks thee early, O my God,
for thy commandments are light on the earth.
I meditated on thy ways, for thou hast become a help to
me.
Early, my Lord, thou shalt hear my voice;
in the morning shall I stand before thee,
and thou shalt look upon me.

Sometimes a prayer speaks very powerfully and meditatively of
the situation for which it was composed. After the terrors and
uncertainties of the dark hours of the night when the soul clings
to God and searches the shadows for his presence, the dawn illu-
minates the world with God's light and chases the fears away.
These prayers deploy Scripture cumulatively in order to praise
God. The morning is a new nativity and the worshipper joins
with the angels of Bethlehem in order to give glory to God.

Coptic Orthodox Vespers Prayers

And he arose from the synagogue and entered Simon's house. And Simon's wife's mother was sick with a high fever, and they made request of him concerning her. And he stood over her and rebuked the fever, and it left her. And immediately she arose and served them. Now when the sun was setting, all those who had anyone sick with various diseases brought them to him; and he laid his hands on every one of them and healed them. And demons also came out of many, crying out and saying, 'Thou art the Christ, the Son of God!' And he, rebuking them, did not allow them to speak, for they knew that he was the Christ.

Glory be to God for ever. ✟ Amen.

May thy saying be concluded in peace. We worship thee, O Christ, together with thy good Father and the Holy Spirit, for thou hast come and saved us.

If the righteous be scarcely saved, where shall I, a sinner, appear? The heaviness of the day and its heat I endured not by reason of my weak nature, but, O thou merciful God, count me with those of the eleventh hour; for, behold, I was conceived in iniquities and in sins did my mother bear me. Wherefore, I presume not to lift my eyes to heaven, but rely on the abundance of thy mercy and thy love towards mankind, crying out and saying: 'O God, forgive me, a sinner, and have mercy on me.'

Glory be to the Father, and to the Son, and to the Holy Spirit.

Make haste, O my Saviour, and lay open thy paternal bosom, for in pleasures and lusts have I spent my life, and behold the day is far spent and passed away. Wherefore I now trust in the abundance of thy never-ending mercy. So forsake not a trembling heart, lacking thy mercy, for unto thee I cry with fear: 'Father, I have sinned against heaven and before thee, and I am not worthy to be called thy son; so make me as one of thine hired servants.'

With diligence did I attempt every transgression, and with eagerness did I strive to commit every sin, and of all suffering and judgement am I worthy. Wherefore, blessed Virgin, prepare for me the way of repentance, for thee I beseech and through thee I intercede and to thee I appeal to help me, lest I be ashamed. And be my attendant at my soul's departure from my body. Overthrow the conspiracies of the enemies, shut fast the gates of Hades lest they devour my soul, O blameless bride of the true Bridegroom.

O Lord, hear us, have mercy on us, and forgive our sins. Lord have mercy (Kyrie eleison). *(41 times)*

Holy, holy, holy, O Lord of Sabaoth,
heaven and earth are full of thy glory and thy majesty.
Have mercy on us, O God the Father Almighty.
O Holy Trinity, have mercy on us.
O Lord of hosts, be thou with us,
for we have no other helper
in our tribulations and necessities but thee.
Loose, remit, and pardon, O God,
our transgressions that we have committed
voluntarily and involuntarily,
consciously and unconsciously,
secretly and openly.
O Lord, remit them for the sake of thy holy Name,
by which we are called,
according to thy mercy, O Lord,
and not according to our sins.

Make us, O Lord, worthy to say with all thanksgiving:
Our Father who art in heaven,
hallowed be thy name.
Thy Kingdom come.
Thy will be done on earth as it is in heaven.
Give us this day our daily bread.
And forgive us our trespasses
as we forgive those who trespass against us.
And lead us not into temptation,
but deliver us from the evil one,
through Christ Jesus our Lord.
For thine is the Kingdom, the power
and the glory, for ever. ✛ Amen.

Then the worshipper prays this prayer:
We thank thee, O our compassionate King, that thou
hast granted us to pass this day in peace, and brought us
thankfully to the evening, and made us worthy to behold
the light until evening.

O God, accept our glorification which we have offered
thee at this time. Deliver us from the intrigues of the
adversary, and annul all his snares set against us, and
grant us a peaceful night free from all pain, restlessness,
fatigue or illusion, that we may pass through it in peace
and chastity, and rise up to give praises and prayers at all
times and everywhere, ascribing glory unto thy holy
Name, together with the Father who is incomprehensible
and without beginning, and the Holy Spirit, the life-giver,
who is equal with thee both now and ever, and unto the
ages of ages. ✛ Amen.

This is very much the evening prayer of one who is wearied by
work and the oppressive heat of the desert world. Early
evening is a time when we are particularly conscious of our
frailty and sinfulness. So it is right and salutary to reflect on
Christ the healer. Like the Prodigal Son we are sickened in our

sinfulness and return to our healing Father who is able to cleanse us of our sins and cares for us in the hours of darkness.

This sequence of prayers begins with the account of Jesus healing Simon's mother-in-law, a story which ends with the confession of the demon that Jesus is indeed the Christ, the Son of God. It is in the context of even the devil recognizing who Jesus is that the rest of these prayers flow. This leads to an extended sequence of self-examination. To be a human being is to be 'diligent in attempting every transgression'. That is the way in which we subvert that for which we were created. But God is merciful, as this sequence recognizes, and the worshipper moves from a consideration of human sinfulness to the grateful appreciation of God's mercy working itself out in us all.

This is monastic prayer and members of community need a particular level of consciousness of their own sinfulness. The gathering gloom after the heat of the desert day is a good time to meditate on these themes.

Coptic Prayer for Laying On Hands

Deacon   Bow your heads to the Lord.

People   Before you, O Lord.

Priest   Your servants, O Lord, who are serving you, entreating your holy name, and bowing down their heads to you: dwell in them, O Lord; walk among them; aid them in every good deed; wake their heart from every vile earthly thought; grant them to live and think of what is pertaining to the living, and understand the things that are yours; through your only-begotten Son, our Lord, God and Saviour, Jesus Christ, unto whom we, and all your people, cry out saying: 'Have mercy upon us, O God, our Saviour.'

People   Lord have mercy. Lord have mercy. Lord have mercy.

Priest   Angel of this sacrifice, flying up to the highest with this hymn, remember us before the Lord, that he may forgive us our sins.

People   ✛ Amen. Alleluia. Glory be to the Father, and to the Son, and to the Holy Spirit, now and for ever, and to the age of ages. ✛ Amen.

We proclaim and say, O our Lord, Jesus Christ, bless the air of heaven, bless the waters of the river, bless the seeds and the herbs; may your mercy and your peace be a fortress unto your people.
Save us and have mercy on us.
Lord have mercy. Lord have mercy.
Lord bless. Bless me.
Forgive me. Say the blessing.

An interesting prayer recalling baptism just after the distribution of communion. Particularly of note is the way in which the prayer looks out of the church into the fields and asks God's blessing on the crops in the fields and the winds and the rivers. Anything which has been achieved in celebrating the Eucharist is not confined to the interior of the church building but has a significance throughout the created order.

Coptic Prayer for Those Who Have Asked for Prayers

Priest Remember, O Lord, those who have bidden us to
remember them . . .

Deacon Pray for all those who have bidden us to
remember them in our prayers and supplications,
each one by his name, that Christ our God may
remember them with goodness at all times and
forgive us our sins.

People Lord have mercy.

Priest In our prayers and supplications which we
offer up unto you, O Lord our God, as in this
particular time of this holy service, those whom
we remember at all times and those who are in the
thoughts of each one of us: let their remembrance,
which is now being made, be to them a firm
shield, prevailing against all afflictions of the
devils and the counsel of evil men.

People Lord have mercy.

Intercessory prayer is a way in which Christians share in the
creative work of God. There is a straightforwardness about
these prayers for those who have asked to be remembered in
church. Particularly intriguing is the idea that the act of remembering is in some way effective as a shield and defence. It is as
if calling to mind has a value in itself as a particular work of
prayer.

Coptic Prayer of St Severus

Said by the priest

O Christ, our God, the fearsome and
incomprehensible power of God the Father,
O you, who sit upon the flaming throne of the Cherubim
and are served by the fiery powers,
yourself a consuming fire, being God:
because of the ineffable act of coming
down and because of your love to mankind,
you did not burn the deceitful betrayer
when he approached you.
But you greeted him with a kiss of friendship,
drawing him to repentance and the comprehension of his
    audacity.

Make us also worthy, O our Master,
in this fearful hour – being of one mind,
with no vestige of a divided heart,
or any other evil –
that we may greet one another with a holy kiss;
and do not condemn us, if we are not entirely clean
(as pleases your goodness)
from the filth of sin and deceit
and the remembrance of evil, which brings forth death.
But you, in your ineffable and undeclarable compassion,
knowing the weakness and the drowning of our creation,
wipe out every defilement of our transgressions,
that this mystery, which is your divinity,
may not be a judgement against us
or a falling into condemnation.

There is a dangerous awfulness about God which makes faithful belief a risky business. This prayer recognizes the power of God, but also his compassion. It is a prayer about confession, repentance and forgiveness. In some respects it recognizes that we are all sinful and only God has a solution to the problem.

Coptic Orthodox Prayers before and after Confession

Before confession

Holy Father, who wishes for the repentance of sinners,
promising to accept them back: look, O Lord, at this
moment, at a sinful soul who had erred and lost her way
in the valley of transgressions for many years, wherein
she was also embittered and wretched through being
removed from the fountain of her salvation. Yet now she
comes forward to you, asking to be cleansed from all the
defilement and filth that sullied her. Accept, and reject
her not, for if you look at her with compassion and deal
with her mercifully she will be cleansed and saved; or if
you neglect her she will perish.

Grant me grace to come near you with faith unshaken
and full of hope to confess my trespasses and despise
them. Let your spirit reprove me for my sins. Enlighten
my heart that I may see how greatly did I err, misbehave
and forsake the way. Grant me determination to forsake
evil that I may be established in your commandments
and live to glorify your holy Name. ✠ Amen.

After confession

I thank your goodness, O lover of man, because you did
not wish my perdition, but have awakened me from my
neglect and guided me to your path. You have brought
me back from the valley of destruction to the safety of
your bosom, so fill me with hope and faith. I have come
to you, a sick person to the Physician, hungry and needy
to the Food of Plenty, thirsty to the Spring of living
water, poor to the Source of riches, sinner to the Saviour,
dead to the Fountain of Life; for you are my salvation,
my healer, my life, my strength, my comfort, my
happiness, and my rest is in you. So help me, protect me
and teach me to put my will in your hands.

There is an elegant beauty about these prayers, an intimate understanding of the need for repentance and a celebration of the gift of forgiveness.

The penitent soul is likened to one roaming aimlessly in the valley of shadows – surely a reference to the Psalms? But once again, this is the prayer of a desert faith where sinfulness and the distancing from God that comes with it is described in terms of being thirsty, parched. The prayer begins in the third person – there is an attempt at being objective, but then the focus shifts. The plea becomes more personal. It is my sins that need cleansing, my parched spirit which needs water. But to deal with it I need strengthening and enlightening, and that can only come from God.

All these themes are tied up in the prayer after confession that retains the intimate tone of the previous prayer. It was the one praying who wandered aimlessly in the valley of destruction but now is restored to health and has drunk deeply of God's abundant and life-giving love.

Ethiopian Anaphora of the Apostles

Celebrant The Lord be with you all.

People   And with your spirit.

Celebrant Give thanks to our God.

People   It is right to give him thanks.

Celebrant Lift up your hearts.

People   We lift them up unto our Lord.

Celebrant We give you thanks, O Lord, by your beloved Son, our Lord Jesus Christ, whom in the latter days you sent for us. He is your Son the Saviour and Redeemer, the angel of your counsel. He is the Word who is from you and through whom you made all things by your will . . . You sent your Son from heaven into the bosom of the Virgin . . . He became flesh, and was born in the womb, and his birth was made known by the Holy Spirit . . . He came and was born of a virgin to fulfil your will and make a holy people for you . . . He stretched out his hands to the Passion, suffering to save the suffering people who have trusted in him. He offered himself by his own will to the Passion that he might destroy death, and burst the bond of Satan, trample on hell, lead forth the saints, confirm the law and make known his resurrection.

He took bread . . . He gave thanks . . . saying: Take, eat, this is my body which is broken for you . . . In the like manner, he took the chalice, saying: Take, drink, this is my blood which is shed for you . . . As often as you will do this, you will do it in remembrance of me.

Now also, O Lord, remembering his death and his resurrection, we offer to you this bread and this chalice, giving thanks to you. You have given us the favour of standing before you and doing your priestly service . . . Uniting all those who are to receive his body and his blood, grant that it may be for their sanctification and that they may therefore receive the fullness of the Holy Spirit, and, being confirmed in the true faith, they may give you glory and praise through your beloved Son, Jesus Christ.

There are fourteen Ethiopian Anaphoras or Eucharistic Prayers used on different occasions throughout the Christian year. Their existence gives us a picture of the development of the Ethiopian eucharistic liturgy across time and space. Some of these prayers are clearly compositions made in Ethiopia. Others hint at a provenance far from the land of Cush – in Syria, Egypt and elsewhere. They are a useful reminder that this form of Christianity, historically and culturally unique, is part of a greater, catholic Church. It is something of which Ethiopian Christians are aware: they are ecumenically minded and were founder members of the World Council of Churches.

This prayer may not seem unfamiliar to Western Christians at least in form and tone. The opening dialogue, sometimes known as the *sursum corda,* is unsurprising, as is, also, the rehearsal of salvation history and the work of Jesus Christ. But what is interesting here is the christological intensity – the careful way in which the work of God in Christ is described and relationships are delineated. The mystery of the incarnation is used to unpack the mystery of our salvation. This is liturgical theology at its most exquisite, when it leads worshippers to pray the theological core of their faith.

Ethiopian Prayer: Pilot of the Soul

Pilot of the soul,
Guide of the righteous,
and Glory of the saints:
grant us, O Lord, eyes of knowledge ever to see thee
and ears also to hearken unto thy word alone.
When our souls have been fulfilled with thy grace,
create in us pure hearts, O Lord,
that we may ever understand thy greatness,
who art good and a lover of men.
O our God, be gracious to our souls,
and grant unto us thy humble servants
who have received thy body and blood,
a pure and steadfast mind,
for thine is the Kingdom, O Lord,
blessed and glorious, Father, Son, and Holy Spirit.

This prayer comes from the end of the Anaphora of Jesus Christ, one of the fourteen Ethiopian Anaphoras. It comes just before the end of the liturgy and has the sense about it of something that is to focus the believer's attention on Christ who will be his or her guide and protector in the days before they next come to church. After a long time in church (and the Ethiopian liturgy lasts many hours) this has a welcome economy and directness about it. It is a prayer that would bear being used in our own Western liturgies instead of our post-eucharistic prayers.

Ethiopian Prayer to the Virgin

Rejoice, O thou of whom we ask healing,
O holy, full of honour, ever-virgin,
parent of God, Mother of Christ:
offer up our prayer on high to thy beloved Son
that he may forgive us our sins.

Rejoice, O thou who didst bear for us
the very Light of Righteousness, even Christ our God.
O Virgin pure, plead for us unto our Lord
that he may have mercy upon our souls
and forgive us our sins.

Rejoice, O Virgin Mary, very Queen;
rejoice, O pride of our kind;
rejoice, O thou that bearest for us Emmanuel our God.
We ask thee to remember us, O true Mediatrix,
before our Lord Jesus Christ,
that he may have mercy upon our souls
and forgive us our sins.

Where does one start to talk about Mary in the Ethiopian tradition? She is everywhere – decorating churches, engraved on crosses, painted on icons or manuscripts. A famous and influential book is a medieval work entitled the *Miracles of Mary* – an extraordinary volume found in large numbers of monasteries – describing a number of apocryphal actions of Mary. A favourite, often gruesomely portrayed, tale is of a cannibal who, having eaten eighty people, did one person a good service by responding to a request for a cup of water. When he died, the cannibal had his soul weighed and was found wanting and destined for hell. But Mary came, and, because of his one good deed, cast her shadow on the balance so that he was granted eternal life with God.

Ethiopian Christians feel close to Mary in an almost physical way. They rely on her intercession in a way that is clear from this prayer. She is the channel through whom human hopes and fears reach Jesus. By the same token she is herself a channel, the means of God becoming human.

Indian Orthodox Prayers for the Morning

Glory be to the Father, and to the Son, and to the Holy
Spirit.

And on us weak and sinful servants
be mercy and compassion in both worlds,
for ever and ever. ✠ Amen.

Creator of the morning,
you who drive out the darkness
and bring light and joy to the creation,
create in us habits of virtue
and drive away from us all the darkness of sin.
With the light, give us joy
by the glorious rays of your grace,
Lord our God, for ever. ✠ Amen.

Indian Orthodox Christians begin their morning office with this
doxology and opening prayer. There are strong echoes of the
Syrian Orthodox tradition of prayer underlying much of Indian
Orthodox worship. Notice how there is a particular 'register' of
language – this is not the sort of language that we might use in
day-to-day speech. The idea of God as Creator, and creation
symbolized in the gift of light, both at the beginning of the
world and every day, is striking. Also striking is the addition to
the opening doxology through which the divine awesomeness
of God is contrasted with the sinfulness and unworthiness of
humanity. But this is not a contrast without hope. On the
contrary, the Christian is aware of living both in this world and
in God's reality. The two intersect, challenging and demanding
much.

The gift of morning light returns our minds and hearts to
God who has made, and is making, what we are and what we
shall be in his time.

Syrian Beginning of the Liturgy of Our Lady

Glory be to the Father, and to the Son, and to the Holy
Spirit.

And upon us, weak and sinful ones,
let mercy and compassion be showered in both worlds,
for ever and ever. ✢ Amen.

Sanctify us by your holiness, O Lord, who are all holy.
You have willed to be born of the holy Virgin Mary
in order that with purity we may commemorate her
and be protected by her prayers.
We offer up to you praise in this her feast,
now, always and for ever. ✢ Amen.

General supplication prayer

Let us all pray and implore the Lord for kindness and
mercy. Merciful Lord, have mercy upon us and help us.
May we be worthy to offer up to you praise,
thanksgiving, glory, adoration and never-ceasing
exaltation, continually, at all times and in all seasons.
   Praise be to the One who is praised and glorified, who
has magnified the remembrance of his Mother in heaven
and on earth, made the remembrance of his saints
known in all the nations and poured the dew of mercy
and compassion on the bones of sleeping believers: to
whom glory and honour are appropriate at this time of
the nocturnal prayer of forgiveness, and in all feasts,
times, ages and through all the days of our life for
evermore. ✢ Amen.

As we celebrate a loving and dear remembrance of her
who is worthy of praise and who is glorified by all the
generations of the earth, the holy, praised, exalted and
ever-virgin, the blessed Mother of God, Mary, we
remember with her the holy prophets, the apostles, the

preachers, the evangelists, the martyrs, the confessors, the just, the priests, the holy fathers, the true pastors, the orthodox doctors, the holy celibates, the righteous, the ascetics, the hermits, the monks and all those who do good works. By their prayers which you hear and their accepted supplications, look upon us with a merciful eye and forgive our debts, pardon our sins and make us and our departed ones worthy of the mansions of the heavenly Jerusalem and the bosom of Abraham, that we may join the company of your saints and be with them and among them. We offer up glory and thanksgiving to you and to your Father and to your living Holy Spirit, for evermore. ✛ Amen.

The beginning of the Liturgy of our Lady places the worshippers in the context of the whole of the Church living and dead. This sense of continuity across time and space is an important part of the Eastern Christian tradition. Perhaps the presence with us of the whole Church of God is something that we have lost in Western Christianity.

But perhaps we have also lost, at least in the more liturgical expressions of worship, the sense of awesome, unalloyed praise: praise that bubbles out of the heart of the worshipping community; a sense of praise that gets things in the right order and in a healthy perspective. Certainly, there is a touch of that overblown language that we call hyperbole, but it is not vacuous or self-indulgent. It has a 'density' appropriate to its subject matter. If some of the higher forms of prayer bring the one praying into a silent engagement with God, this is not transferable into a liturgical setting (much though that might be attractive at times). Some other strategy needs adopting with regard to the sort of language we use in worship. This is a good example – words, and the ideas with which they are associated, piled up on each other like books in the most glorious of second-hand bookshops, a musty exuberance asking the worshipper to make an effort, search and look.

Syrian Anaphora of St James

The celebrant, extending and elevating his hands, says aloud:
Upward, where Christ sits on the right hand of God the Father, let our thoughts, minds and hearts be at this hour.

People They are with the Lord God.

Celebrant Let us give thanks to the Lord in awe.

People It is meet and right.

Celebrant Truly it is meet and right to thank, worship and praise the Creator of the whole world, he whom the heavenly hosts, corporeal and incorporeal, glorify; the sun, the moon and all the stars; the earth, the seas and the firstborn inscribed in the heavenly Jerusalem; angels and archangels, celestial virtues, principalities, thrones, dominions, powers, the many-eyed Cherubim and the six-winged Seraphim who, covering their faces and feet, fly to one another, chanting the thrice holy, crying and saying: Holy.

People Holy, holy, holy, Lord God Almighty; heaven and earth are full of his glories. Hosanna in the highest. Blessed is he who came and will come in the Name of the Lord. Hosanna in the highest.

In truth you are holy and you make holy, O King of the worlds, and holy is your Son, our Lord Jesus Christ, and holy too is your Holy Spirit who searches out hidden things. You created man out of earth and placed him in paradise, and when he transgressed your commandment, you did not leave him straying, but guided him by the prophets, and in the fullness of time you sent your only-begotten Son into the world, who when he had taken flesh of the Holy Spirit and of the Virgin Mary, renewed your image in us which was worn out.

When he, the sinless One, was prepared to accept voluntary death for us sinners, he took bread into his holy hands and when he had given thanks, he blessed ✠ ✠ and sanctified ✠ and broke and gave to his holy disciples, and said: Take, eat of it. This is my body which for you and for many is broken and given for the remission of sins and for eternal life.

People   ✠ Amen.

Celebrant   Likewise, he took the cup and when he had given thanks, he blessed ✠ ✠ and sanctified ✠ and gave it to his holy disciples, and said: Take, drink of it, all of you. This is my blood which for you and for many is shed and given for the remission of sins and for eternal life.

People   ✠ Amen.

Celebrant   Do this in remembrance of me when you partake of this sacrament, commemorating my death and my resurrection until I come.

People   Your death, our Lord, we commemorate, your resurrection we confess and your second coming we wait for. May your mercy be upon us all.

Celebrant   While we remember, O Lord, your death and your resurrection on the third day, your ascension into heaven, your sitting at the right hand of God the Father and your second coming whereby you will judge the world in righteousness and reward everyone according to his deeds; on account of this, we offer you this bloodless sacrifice so that you may not deal with us according to our debts, nor reward us according to our sins, but, according to your abundant mercies, blot out the sins of your servants for your people. Your inheritance make supplication unto you and through you to your Father, saying:

People   Have mercy upon us, O God, Father Almighty.
We glorify you, we bless you,
we worship you and we beseech you.
O Lord our God, have compassion
and mercy upon us, O Good One.

Celebrant We also, O Lord, your weak and sinful servants,
offer you thanksgiving and acknowledge your
loving-kindness unto all and for all.

People   We glorify you, we bless you,
we worship you, O Lord God,
and we beseech you for mercy.
Have mercy upon us.

Deacon   How awful is this hour and how dreadful is this
moment, my beloved, wherein the Holy Spirit
from the topmost heights takes wing and descends
and hovers and rests upon this Eucharist here
present and sanctifies it. Be calm and in awe, while
standing and praying.

People   May peace be with us, and tranquillity in all of us.

There can be few, if any, Churches which have quite as rich a collection of eucharistic worship as the Syrian Orthodox. With no fewer than eighty Anaphoras or Eucharistic Prayers it is an extraordinary corpus of liturgy. It would be tempting to include a number of examples, but there is really only room for one.

The Syrian Church often calls its liturgy the Holy Qu'bono (Oblation or Sacrifice), and the whole service is rich in symbolism both of word and action. This Anaphora, ascribed to St James, has a shape that Western Christians may well recognize. What is distinctive is the sense of the immanence of the sacred world: the Eucharist is celebrated in the company of the whole host of heaven. This is something that we have seen articulated in different ways in many of these prayers from the East.

There is an attractive, if slightly unusual, addition to the *sursum corda*, which comes across as rather more cumbersome in this English translation than in Syriac, where it has a more poetic and expansive sense. This gives way to an invocation of the hosts of heaven which draws heavily on Isaiah as a source and model for its imagery.

The rehearsal of salvation history is probably more familiar to Western Christians now that Eucharistic Prayers with a more Eastern shape are included in our books of liturgies. But there are still moments when one is brought up short by an unfamiliar set of concepts or an intriguing way of expressing things. The arresting moments during the liturgy make us view the whole with new eyes.

Syrian Canon of the Faithful Brethren

Deacon Again, we remember all our faithful and true
Christian brethren who have urged and entreated
our humble and weak selves to remember them at
this hour and at this time: and on behalf of all
those who are fallen into all kinds of hard
temptations and who take refuge in you, Lord
God Almighty, and for their salvation and speedy
visitation by you; for this city sustained by God
and for the concord and prosperity of all its
faithful dwellers that they may attain
righteousness. Let us beseech the Lord.

People Kyrie eleison.

Deacon Remember, O Lord, all those whom we have
mentioned and those whom we have not
mentioned and receive their sacrifices into the
expanses of your heaven. Bestow on them the joy
of salvation and make them worthy of your help.
Strengthen them with your power and arm them
with your might; for you are merciful, and to you
we offer up glory and praise, and to your only-
begotten Son, and to your Holy Spirit, all holy,
good, adorable and life-giving, who is of one
substance with you, now, always and for ever.

People ✢ Amen.

I am never alone in my worship. I am never just responsible for
myself, my own faithfulness and faithlessness. I am a part of
something greater and more mysterious. I have a responsibility
for its unity, its continuity and to remember everyone when I
bring my gift to the altar.

Syrian Epiclesis: The Invocation of the Holy Spirit

Celebrant   Have mercy upon us, O God the Father, and send
upon these offerings your Holy Spirit, the Lord
who is equal to you and to the Son in dominion,
reign and eternal substance; who spoke through
your Old and New Testaments; and descended in
the likeness of a dove on our Lord Jesus Christ in
the Jordan River and in the likeness of tongues of
fire on the apostles in the Upper Room.

Answer me, O Lord;
answer me, O Lord;
answer me, O Lord;
O Good One, have compassion and mercy upon
me.

People   Kyrie eleison. Kyrie eleison. Kyrie eleison.

Celebrant   So that, by his indwelling, he [the Holy Spirit] may
make this bread the life-giving body ✠, the
redeeming body ✠ and the body ✠ of Christ our
God.

People   ✠ Amen.

Celebrant   And may he [the Holy Spirit] perfect this cup into
the blood ✠ of the new covenant, the redeeming
blood ✠ and the blood ✠ of Christ our God.

People   ✠ Amen.

Celebrant   So that they [holy mysteries] may sanctify the
souls and bodies of those who partake of them for
the bearing of the fruit of good deeds; for the
confirmation of the holy Church which is founded
on the rock of faith and is invincible to the gates
of Sheol. Deliver her from heretical offences to the

end that she may offer up glory and praise to you and to your only-begotten Son and your Holy Spirit, all holy, good, adorable and life-giving, who is of one substance with you, now, always and for ever.

People ✣ Amen.

After the words of institution of the Eucharist the Holy Spirit is called upon to come down and sanctify the bread and wine which have been offered on the altar. This is known as the epiclesis, from the Greek word for invocation. We should not see in this prayer of invocation any sense that this is the moment of consecration, the point in time when bread becomes flesh and wine blood. Eastern liturgies resist this sense of time. Rather, it is a celebration of the continuing activity of the Spirit in the Old Testament, at Christ's baptism and in this Eucharist. Moreover, this example reminds us of the activity of the Spirit preserving and guiding the Church in truth.

Syrian Evening Prayer

I call upon you, Lord; hear me!
Give heed to my words and answer me.
Let my prayer be like incense in your sight,
my uplifted hands be like an evening sacrifice.
Lord, set a guard at my mouth, a sentry at the door of
    my lips,
that my heart may not turn to evil and indulge in the
    deeds of wickedness.
Let me not sit at the table of the wicked.
Let the righteous man teach me, let him reprove me,
but the oil of the wicked shall not anoint my head,
my prayer is against their evil deeds.
When their judges are thrown down in stony places,
they shall hear my words, for they are sweet.
Their bones are scattered at the mouth of the grave
like the plough that breaks the earth.
I lift up my eyes to you, Lord.
I put my trust in you, do not leave my soul destitute.
Keep me away from the hands of the proud who have
    laid snares for me.
Let the wicked fall into their own traps, while I go
    unharmed.
While my soul was in agony, I cried to the Lord with my
    voice;
with all my voice I made supplication.
I poured out my affliction before him;
I told him all my troubles.
When my spirit was overwhelmed within me, then you
    knew my path.
They have hidden snares for me in the way I have to
    walk.
I looked to the right, but there was no one who knew
    me; no one cared for my soul.
I cried to you, O Lord! I said,
you are my refuge and my portion in the land of the
    living.

Attend to my supplication; for I am in distress.
Deliver me from my persecutors, for they are stronger
than me.
Lead me forth from prison that I may praise your name.
The righteous shall wait for me because you will answer
me.
Your word is a lamp to my feet and a light for my path.
I have sworn and have determined to keep your holy
decrees.
I am made to be low, Lord. Give me life according to
your word.
Lord, be pleased with the words of my lips and teach me
your decrees.
My life is always in your hands, I do not forget your
laws.
The wicked have set traps for me, but I have not strayed
from your commands.
I treasure up your testimonies. Truly they are the joy of
my heart.
Incline my heart to keep your commands, in truth, for
ever.
Praise the Lord, all you nations. Praise him, all you
people.
Great is his goodness for us. Truly, the Lord's goodness
is for ever.
To you belongs praise, O God.
O Lord, listen to our prayers with mercy and answer
them with compassion.
May God accept, and be pleased in our worship and
prayers and be gracious to us.

Offering of incense

Lord, let our prayers be like a pleasing incense before
you.
Let them rise to the highest like an offering of fragrance.

As you are pleased in the offer of incense,
accept our worship, prayers, supplications and praises,
without counting our unworthiness, and grant our
    petitions.

For the intercession of the Mother of God

O Virgin Mother!
Shield us from all menaces that confront us
and keep far from us the stormy winds and tides of this
    world.
O Mother!
Since you have acceptance in the presence of God,
pray that your intercession may grant us forgiveness and
    mercy,
heal the sick, bring relief to the afflicted
and the return to us peacefully of those who are away.

For the intercession of saints

Martyrs!
As in the time of deluge, when the righteous Noah
protected the beasts that entered with him into the ark,
let your intercession protect us from the tides and stormy
    winds that encircle this world.

For the intercession of a patron saint

St [Name]!
Your grace has astonished the heavenly beings.
Your glorious name is praised on earth among us.
Your good deeds have been counted worthy by your
    Lord Jesus Christ,
and he has revered and upheld your memory.
May your prayers be a refuge to us.

Prayer of repentance

O God,
the lover of those who are unblemished and upright,
    grant us perfection in our hearts.
Remove from us all evil and malicious thoughts.
O Lord, open to us your merciful door, as you did to the
    thief.
Accept our repentance as you accepted the penance of
    the tax-collector and the sinful woman.
O Lord, you are merciful and pleased with those who
    turn to you in repentance,
as you graciously pardoned Peter who came to you after
    he had denied you.
Lord, cleanse us from our sins and follies.
O Lord! We, the sinful, grieve about your dispassionate
    last judgement.
When the great books of account are opened and our
    sins are read, let your grace strengthen us and let your
    mercy help us.
Let our sins be pardoned.
O Lord! We acknowledge our sins, have mercy on us.

For the faithful departed

Lord!
Grant good remembrance to the faithful departed
who have received your atoning body and blood.
Lord Jesus Christ,
when you come gloriously with the company of angels,
let our departed ones stand before you with praises.

O Lord!
Enable us to take part in the memorial
of your Mother, prophets, apostles, martyrs and all saints.

By their prayers, protect the living,
and in your mercy sanctify our faithful departed.

Special prayers for the day may be said here.

Lord Jesus Christ,
do not close the door of your mercy on our faces.
Lord, we confess that we are sinners: have mercy upon
us.
O Lord, your love made you descend from your place to
us,
that by your death, our death was abolished: have mercy
upon us.

Evening prayer in the Syrian tradition brings together psalms, hymns and prayers in a rich mixture. The opening prayer of this selection is a catena of scriptural quotations whose cumulative effect is to prepare the worshipper for the service that will follow. The lighting of a lamp and the offering of incense are both normal features of the Syrian tradition. The prayer for the offering of incense reproduced here has an elegant economy, springing from its Old Testament roots, as an invocation and supplication on behalf of the worshipper.

Similarly, in the invocation of the saints and of Mary, prayers begin with the remembrancing of an Old Testament text before developing to a simple petition or the articulation of a single hope.

Syrian Homily of St Jacob of Serugh

O Father of truth, behold your Son, the well-pleasing
　　sacrifice to you,
as you accept him who died for me, so may I be forgiven
　　through him.
Receive this offering from my hands and be reconciled
　　with me.
And do not remember the sins I committed before your
　　greatness.
Behold his blood is shed on Golgotha by the wicked, and
　　it is pleading for me.
For my sake, accept my petition.
If you weigh how much are my debts and how much is
　　your mercy,
your compassion is heavier than the mountains that are
　　weighed by you.
Look at the sins and look at the offering for them –
the offering and the sacrifice are much greater than the
　　debts.
Because I sinned, your beloved One endured the nails
　　and the spear.
Sufficient are his sufferings to reconcile you, and by them
　　shall I live.
Glory be to the Father, who delivered his Son for our
　　salvation.
Adoration to the Son, who died on the cross and gave
　　life to all of us.
Thanks be to the Spirit, who began and fulfilled the
　　mystery of our salvation.
O Trinity, exalted above all, have mercy on us all.

Jacob of Serugh is a Syrian saint who lived in the fifth century
and died as Bishop of Batnae in 521. His life coincided with
considerable persecution of Syrian Christians at the hands of
Persians. He is known for his series of metrical homilies; this is
part of one, which has been retained in the Syrian rite.

It is a theological meditation on salvation and our place in the divine economy. The early part contrasts our sinfulness with the action of Christ in the passion, before reaching a trinitarian conclusion.

Syrian Hymn before Communion

I was a lost and wandering sheep.
The Church responded, saying:
I was scattered and dispersed.
Lo! My Shepherd went out in search of me, and found
  me.
He carried me and put me on his shoulder,
and brought me into his fold of life;
he set before me the table of life:
his atoning body and blood,
so that, by its means, my children and I together
might be always sustained.
Therefore, my children and I,
with one accord, cry out to him, saying:
Holy, holy, holy are you, O Son,
who gave us your body and blood.
Holy are you, O Son of God;
blessed be your honour from your dwelling-place.

This hymn before communion is a good example of the simple yet creative use of biblical themes to reflect prayerfully and creatively on the saving work of God. In the context of the period of reflection just before receiving the Eucharist, it has an added quality of transparency. The believer is a sheep, the one that was lost, and is being brought back to the fold on the shoulders of Christ.

Syrian Hymn of Mar Ephrem the Syrian for Compline

Lord have mercy upon us,
kindly accept our prayers;
grant us mercy and redemption,
from thy treasury above.

Let me, Lord, stand before thee,
wakeful, I'd keep my watch;
should I fall into the hands of sleep,
protect me from sleep's sinfulness.

If I do wrong while awake,
mercifully absolve me;
if I err in my sleep,
in mercy, grant redemption.

By thy cross ✢ of submission
grant me, Lord, a restful sleep;
drive vain and evil dreams,
O my Lord, far from thy servant.

Through the night conduct me, Lord,
peaceful sleep give thou to me;
let not wroth and foul thoughts,
O Lord, govern me at all.

O Lord, thy servant I am:
guard my body while I sleep;
keep thy bright angels' guard,
O my Lord, by my side.

Christ, may thy life-abiding
holy body that I ate
keep away from my heart
evil desires that destroy.

While I sleep in this night,
may thy holy blood guard me;
be thou always redeemer,
for I am thine image.

Thy hand shaped me, O Lord;
shadow me with thy right hand,
let thy mercy be a fortress
shielding me all around.

While my body silent lies,
may thy power keep vigil;
let me sleep in thy presence,
be like the rising incense.

Thy Mother who didst bear thee,
by her prayers for me, O Lord,
let not evil touch my bed
while I slumber in this night.

By thy pleasing sacrifice
that absolved me from my distress,
keep far from me the wicked one
that keeps troubling me.

By thy kindness, O my Lord,
thy promise in me is fulfilled;
by thy holy cross ✞, O Lord,
protect my life completely.

Thou who art pleased in me,
feeble and sinful servant I am,
may I praise thy mercy,
when I wake up from my sleep.

May thy servant know thy will;
in thy true loving kindness,
grant me, O Lord, thy mercy
so that I may walk with thee.

Jesus Christ, O my Lord,
grant to us thy servants
an evening filled with peace
and a night of graceful sleep.

True light thou art, O Lord,
praise we thy bright glory.
We children of thy light
praise thee for ever more.

O Saviour of mankind,
thy servants praise thy mercy;
as we do in this world,
may it be in heaven above.

Praise to thee, O my Lord;
praise to thee, O my Saviour;
praise a thousand thousandfold;
praise we thee, O Jesus Christ.

Thou who dost receive our prayers,
thou who grantest supplications,
heed thy servants' prayers,
kindly grant our petitions.

Kyrie eleison. Kyrie eleison. Kyrie eleison.

Ephrem the Syrian was a deacon living and working in Nisibis in
the fourth century. His greatest gift to the Church is a corpus of
devotional and expository hymns, many of which are still used in
the Syrian Church even today. Ephrem is capable of writing
hymns of extraordinary poetic and metaphoric complexity. The
one reproduced here is straightforward compared to many of his
works, and has a simple structure. But it has an attractive open-
ness. The worshipper, preparing for the hours of darkness,
commits him- or herself into the hands of God.

Syrian Introduction to Prayer

Leader   Holy art thou, O God.

People   Holy art thou, Almighty;
holy art thou, Immortal;
✝ crucified for us, have mercy on us. *(3 times)*

Leader   Lord, have mercy upon us.

People   Lord, be kind and have mercy;
Lord, accept our prayers and worship
and have mercy on us.

Leader   Glory be to thee, O God;

People   Glory be to thee, O Creator;
Glory be to thee, O Christ,
the King who dost pity sinners, thy servants.
Barekhmor.

The Lord's Prayer (Matthew 6.9–13; Luke 11.2–4)

Leader   Our Father, who art in heaven,

People   Hallowed be thy Name.
Thy Kingdom come;
thy will be done on earth, as it is in heaven.
Give us this day our daily bread:
and forgive us our trespasses
as we forgive those who trespass against us.
Lead us not into temptation,
but deliver us from the evil one;
for thine is the Kingdom, the power and the glory
for ever and ever. ✝ Amen.

Hail Mary (Luke 1.28–42)

Leader   Hail Mary, full of grace.

People   Our Lord is with thee.
Blessed art thou among women,
and blessed is the fruit of thy womb,
our Lord, Jesus Christ.
O Virgin Saint Mary, O Mother of God,
pray for us sinners, now and at all times,
and at the hour of our death. ✠ Amen

Used in a wide variety of services, this sequence of Trisagion, Lord's Prayer and Hail Mary is learned by heart at an early age. *Barekhmor* is the Syriac for 'Bless my Lord'.

Syrian Introduction to the Lord's Prayer

O God and Father of our Lord Jesus Christ, who are
blessed by the Cherubim, hallowed by the Seraphim and
exalted by thousands of thousands and myriads of
myriads of the spiritual hosts; you who sanctify and
make perfect the offerings and the ripe fruits, which have
been offered for a sweet-smelling fragrance, sanctify also
our bodies, souls and spirits so that with a pure heart
and a face unashamed we may call upon you, O God,
the heavenly Father, and pray, saying: Our Father, who
art in heaven.

The Lord's Prayer

People   Hallowed be thy Name.
             Thy Kingdom come;
             thy will be done, on earth as it is in heaven.
             Give us this day our daily bread.
             And forgive us our trespasses
             as we forgive those who trespass against us.
             And lead us not into temptation,
             but deliver us from evil.
             For thine is the Kingdom, the power and the
                  glory,
             for ever and ever. ✠ Amen.

Celebrant Yes, Lord our God, let us not enter into intolerable
             temptation, but deliver us from the evil one,
             making a way of escaping from temptation; and to
             you we raise glory and thanks and to your only-
             begotten Son and to your Holy Spirit, all-holy,
             good, adorable and life-giving, who is of one
             substance with you, now, always and for ever.

People   ✠ Amen. *Barekhmor* [Bless my Lord].

Celebrant Peace be with you all.

People	And with your spirit.
Deacon	Before receiving these divine and holy mysteries that have been offered, let us bow down our heads before the merciful Lord.
People	Before you, our Lord and our God. Unto you your servants, who are awaiting your rich mercies, have bowed down their heads. Send forth, O Lord, your blessings and sanctify our bodies, souls and spirits, and make us worthy to partake of the life-giving mysteries of Christ, our Saviour, and we will offer glory and thanks to you and to your only-begotten Son and to your Holy Spirit, all holy, good, adorable and life-giving, who is of one substance with you, now, always and for ever.
People	✛ Amen. *Barekhmor*.
Celebrant	Peace be with you all.
People	And with your spirit.

Many Eastern Churches retain quite elaborate introductions to the Lord's Prayer just before the distribution of communion. The Syrian Church is no exception. Once again, the worshipper is left in no doubt that he or she is worshipping with the whole company of heaven.

120

Syriac Liturgical Supplications

Celebrant Let us all pray and implore the Lord for kindness . . .

Praise be to the three holy Persons, one true God,
who dwells in the Holy of Holies in his
 incomprehensible secrecy;
who is ministered to by the holy hosts with a spiritual
 service
and who accepted by his abounding grace to be served
 by mortals;
who is the Giver of presents and divine gifts,
the Adorner of pontiffs and Perfecter of priests;
who reveals the symbols and fulfils the commandments;
the Accepter of the sacrifices and Granter of the requests;
to him are due praise and honour at this time of the
 celebration of the Eucharist
and at all feasts, seasons, hours, times and all the days of
 our life for ever and ever.

O Mighty, Strong, Powerful and Glorious Lord,
arise and help us and deliver us from the evil one and his
 forces
by your strength and your exalted arm.
You, O Lord, by virtue of your grace and abundant
 mercies,
became incarnate of the holy Virgin Mary,
and by your love towards mankind you put on a body
 for our sake.

O Lord, our Lord, we beseech you
by the throne in heaven which solemnly carries your
 majesty;
by the four faces of the creatures that are bound to your
 chariot;
by the assemblies of the angels and the archangels who
 glorify your Godhead;

by the ranks of the Cherubim who bless, praise and
magnify your might;
by the six-winged Seraphim who cry out, and say:
'Holy, holy, holy are you, O Lord, in your holiness';
by all the hosts, orders and ranks who stand and serve
your awesomeness and your being begotten in the
womb which carried you:
cast us not away from your presence, but show us the
path of life and salvation wherein we may walk to the
Kingdom.

Grant, O my Lord, that we give thanks to your grace,
pray and beseech your kindness.
Our Lord Jesus Christ, have mercy upon us.
Our Lord Jesus Christ, help us.
Our Lord Jesus Christ, deliver us from our enemies.
Our Lord Jesus Christ, under the wings of your cross,
protect us.
Our Lord Jesus Christ, from our fall into sin, lift us up.
Our Lord Jesus Christ, out of the pitfall and the gulf of
afflictions, raise us.
Our Lord Jesus Christ, from all the snares of the
adversary, preserve us.
Our Lord Jesus Christ, from all evil thoughts, deliver us.
Our Lord Jesus Christ, from defilement and blasphemy,
save us.
Our Lord Jesus Christ, from the filth and the stain of
foul deeds, wash us.
Our Lord Jesus Christ, from wickedness and stains,
purify us.
Our Lord Jesus Christ, with your goodness and your
blessings, satisfy us.
Our Lord Jesus Christ, from your treasure which is full
of mercy and compassion, enrich us.
Our Lord Jesus Christ, in your heavenly resting place
which is full of joy, gladden us.
Our Lord Jesus Christ, make us rejoice with the guests
and the invited ones of your Kingdom.

Our Lord Jesus Christ, with the just and the righteous
  who pleased you, invite us.
Our Lord Jesus Christ, with the lambs who stand at your
  right hand, place us.
Our Lord Jesus Christ, with the elect ones and saints,
  make us to shine on the day when your majesty is
  manifest.

Our Lord Jesus Christ, in that spiritual banquet, at your
  right hand, make us sit, so that, with our departed
  ones and with all the faithful departed, we may raise
  to you,
O my Lord, praise and thanksgiving, and to your Father
  and to your Holy Spirit, now, always and for ever.

These liturgical supplications are vast in their scope. It is hard
to see anything like this being used in a service in the Western
Church. And yet there is a real sense of majesty here: an accu-
mulation of words and images of theological truths and the
conceits of art. Read carefully they spin the mind off in creative
directions and the believer is under no illusion about the rich
seam of faith of which they are a part.

   But the prayer works through a carefully contrived structure,
beginning with an invocation of God as Trinity – distant and
ineffable. One is not sure whether pontiffs need really to be
adorned, though some obviously like to be. Certainly priests
(and, indeed, the entire people of God) need to be perfected.
The prayer moves from the adoration of God, via the incarnation in the womb of the Virgin Mary, to a consideration and
invocation of Christ. The believer sets all his or her inadequa-
cies before Christ and asks for his assistance. All the time there
are lines which trigger reminiscences of Christ's parables
(wedding guests, sheep and goats etc.), and close reading
reveals these petitions to be extraordinarily complex and
detailed compositions.

Syriac Post-Communion Homily of St Jacob

The Lord whom the seraphs fear to look at,
the same you behold in bread and wine on the altar.
The lightning-clothed hosts are burned if they see him in
    his brilliance,
yet the contemptible dust partakes of him with confidence.
The Son's mysteries are fire among the heavenly beings,
Isaiah bears witness with us to having seen them.
These mysteries which were in the Divinity's bosom,
are distributed to Adam's children on the altar.
The altar is fashioned like the Cherubim's chariot,
and is surrounded by the heavenly hosts.
On the altar is laid the body of God's Son,
and Adam's children carry it solemnly on their hands.
Instead of a man clad in linen, stands the [priest],
and distributes alms [the Eucharist] among the needy.
If envy existed among the angels,
the Cherubim would have envied men.
Where Zion set up the cross to crucify the Son,
there grew up the tree that gave birth to the Lamb.
Where nails were driven in the Son's hands,
there Isaac's hands were bound for an offering.
Welcome to the priest, who carries the mysteries of his
    Lord,
and with his right hand distributes life to men.
Welcome to the priest, who carries a pure censer,
and with its fragrance makes the world sweet and
    pleasant.
Welcome to the priest, whom the Holy Spirit did raise up,
and on his tongue bears the keys to the house of God.
Welcome to the priest, who binds man in the depth
    below,
and the Lord binds him in heaven on high. Halleluiah.
Welcome to the priest, who unbinds men on earth,
and the Lord unbinds him in the highest. Kyrie eleison.
Praise be to the Lord. His mercy upon you and
    absolution for me.

Here is a moment of quiet contemplation of all that has been achieved in the Eucharist, from the pen of Jacob of Serugh (d. 521). Jacob was a Syriac writer who was known as 'The Flute of the Holy Spirit', and wrote many metrical homilies like the one extracted here. We have seen elsewhere that Isaiah's vision of God in the Temple (Isaiah 6) is frequently used as a starting point by writers in the Syriac tradition. The saint begins here by stating the ineffable nature of God, and draws on Old Testament references to strengthen his point. It is the same all-powerful and dangerous God who is available to us in the Eucharist. And the Eucharist itself is paralleled with the cleansing coal that the seraph places on Isaiah's lips (Isaiah 6.6). The parallels between the Old Testament and the New are tightly drawn, each illuminating the other. And the parallelism is extended to that between our earthly reality and that of heaven. But on the way the worshipper has travelled over a good deal of territory. Much of this liturgy presumes a significant level of familiarity with Scripture on the part of the believer. This is common in the Christian East where Christians tend to retain a significant level of material in their memories.

Syriac Praise of the Cherubim

Leader   ☩ Blessed be the glory of the Lord, from his place for ever.

People   Holy and glorious Trinity, have mercy upon us.

Leader   ☩ Blessed be the glory of the Lord, from his place for ever.

People   Holy and glorious Trinity, have mercy upon us.

Leader   ☩ Blessed be the glory of the Lord, from his place for ever and ever.

People   Holy and glorious Trinity, have compassion and mercy upon us.

Leader   You are holy and glorious for ever.

People   You are holy and glorious for ever, and your name is blessed for ever.

Leader   Glory to you, our Lord.

People   Glory to you, our Lord. Glory to you, our hope for ever.

A moment of exuberant dialogue from the Syriac Orthodox liturgy. Reflecting, albeit distantly, the praise of the Cherubim described by Isaiah, it is a moment of unalloyed praise. The people bless the triune God and ask for mercy. Western Christians, more used to a sparser liturgy, are sometimes bemused by the Eastern Christian's love of repetition. But it is not repetition without meaning; it builds a structure of praise, a blissful dialogue of affirmation.

Syrian Prayer of Divine Dispensation

The memorial of our Lord, our God and our Saviour
    Jesus Christ,
and all of his redemptive dispensations on our behalf;
especially the message of the angel;
his birth in the flesh, his baptism in the Jordan River and
    his fast of forty days,
his voluntary sufferings and his lifting up on the cross,
his life-giving death and his revered burial,
his glorious resurrection, his ascension into heaven
and his sitting on the right hand of God the Father.

We, moreover, remember, at this time,
over this Eucharist set before us,
first of all, our father Adam, our mother Eve,
the Holy Mother of God, Mary,
the prophets, the apostles, the preachers, the evangelists,
the martyrs, the confessors, the just ones,
the priests, the holy fathers, the true pastors,
the orthodox doctors, the anchorites, the monks,
those who are standing and praying with us
and all those who ever since have pleased you
from Adam and Eve until this day.

We also remember our fathers, our brethren and our
    masters,
who have taught us correctly the word of truth;
our own departed ones and all the faithful departed,
particularly and especially those who are from our own
    blood,
those who took part in the building of this place;
all those who took part and are still taking part in
    supporting this place,
as well as all those who have partnership with us,
in word or in deed, in little or in much.

The prayers of other Christian traditions often send us back to our own prayer books with fresh eyes. A common factor of much praying within the Church of the Christian East is the sense that the Church that is doing the praying is not confined to the experienced world of the here and now. The Church is much bigger and more interesting than that.

This prayer invites the worshipper to make connections, across time and through eternity. It begins with a whistle-stop account of Jesus' saving activity. Then, almost as breathless, there is an invocation of the faithful across human time, from Adam and Eve until the present day and the present congregation. Finally, there is a prayer inviting the worshipper to consider and pray for all those who have brought them to faith. It is a wholehearted commemoration of benefaction – energetic and yet considerate. Worshippers acknowledge their connectedness to others in a strong image of the Church as an eternal community of believers.

But it certainly doesn't paint a picture of an institution helplessly backward-facing and mired in the past. There is something more here, something healthy and positive. History and tradition are the bedrock of present faith, not its shackles.

Syrian Prayer of Thanksgiving

Celebrant   We give thanks to you, O Lord, for the abundance of your mercy, by which we have been made worthy to partake of your heavenly table. May we not be condemned for receiving your holy mysteries, but being worthy, may we be in fellowship with your Holy Spirit and find a portion and inheritance with all the righteous who have been from the beginning; and we raise glory and praise to you and to your only-begotten Son and to your Holy Spirit, all-holy, good, adorable and life-giving, who is of one substance with you, now, always and for ever.

People   ✛ Amen.

Celebrant   Peace be unto you all.

People   And with your spirit.

Deacon   After having received these holy and divine mysteries, that have been given, let us again bow down our heads before the merciful Lord.

People   Before you, our Lord and our God.

Celebrant   O great and wonderful God, who descended from heaven and came down for the salvation of our human race, have compassion and mercy upon us so that, at all times, we may glorify you and God the Father who begot you and your Holy Spirit, all holy, good, adorable and life-giving, who is of one substance with you, now, always and for ever.

People   ✛ Amen.

At the heart of all worship is praise. Simply put and beautifully enacted, this is the theme and substance of these prayers after communion. But let us stop and consider them a little more carefully. There is a Pauline warning to Christians to be wary of receiving communion when not in an honourable spiritual state. And this is the basis for the concern shown at the beginning of this prayer. But the thrust of the argument does not end there. For from the presumption of worthiness springs the hope of a table fellowship in heaven. Some have talked about this as the eschatological table fellowship – and there is a sense in the Synoptic Gospels of Jesus talking about the Kingdom of God as a great banquet. But this is seen in combination with the theological reality of God in Christ. For us in the West the insistence on the formal language of theology may seem alien; for the Eastern Christian it is a joyful acclamation of who God is.

There is then a recapitulation of the *sursum corda* dialogue which began the Eucharistic Prayer, a neat and somehow appropriate touch before the concluding prayers of praise.

Syrian Prayer of the Ninth Hour

Praise be to you O God,
who give life to the dead.
Praise be to you O God,
who grant resurrection to the entombed.
We praise you and glorify your Father
who did send you and the Holy Spirit.
O Lord, one of Trinity, who by your own will
stayed in the tomb for three days,
give resurrection to our departed ones,
for they were saved by your precious blood.

O merciful Lord, renew your creation on the day of
   resurrection.
O Lord, grant rest and comfort to our beloved departed
   ones who have lived and died with hope in you.
O Lord, grant rest to our faithful departed in the bosom
   of Abraham, Isaac and Jacob.
May the souls and bodies together cry aloud and say:
glory be to the one who has come and is to come to
   resurrect the departed. ✛ Amen.

This is a prayer of the evening, and it has that reflective, almost melancholic air to it. The focus is on death, both human dying and the death of Christ and his entombment. The language is delicate, treading softly through the mystery of salvation. But as it unfolds the role of Christ in granting salvation to those who were in the tomb, there is a crescendo of expectant hope.

In the whole of the Christian East the idea of Christ extending salvation to Adam and Eve and all the souls in hell has significant currency both as a theological motif and as an inspirational source for visual and poetic creations.

Syrian Prayers of Confession and Absolution

Upon confession of sin before the priest

I confess to God the Father Almighty, and to his beloved
Son, Jesus Christ, and to the Holy Spirit, in the presence
of our Lady the Virgin, ever sacred in her virginity, and
all the holy angels, of Michael, of Gabriel, both chief of
angels, and St John the Baptist, of the holy apostles
St Peter and St Paul, the twenty-four prophets, the
twelve apostles, the four evangelists and the seventy-two
sent forth.

I confess the holy faith of the three Ecumenical Councils
of Nicaea, Constantinople and Ephesus in the most
noble priesthood ascribed to you, Father Priest, by which
you loose and bind.
  I have sinned through all my senses, both inwardly
and outwardly, in word, in deed and in thought. My sin
is great, very great, and I repent of it most sincerely,
purposing not to fall again into the same ever, preferring
death rather than embrace sin. And I ask you, by the
authority of the sacred priesthood, that you absolve me
and forgive, asking God to pardon me through his grace.
✚ Amen.

Prayer of absolution for the laity

*The priest lays his right hand on the head of the penitent
and says:*
May God have mercy upon you, and may he guide you
to everlasting life through the authority of priesthood
which was entrusted by our Lord Jesus Christ to his
disciples who, in turn, entrusted it to their successors
until it was given me; I who am weak and sinful absolve
you, brother [sister], of all the sins that you have
confessed and of which you repent, as well as of all the
transgressions which have escaped your memory, in the

132

name of the Father ✠, amen, and of the Son ✠, amen,
and of the Holy Spirit ✠, for everlasting life. ✠ Amen.

One of the chief points of interest in these prayers is the sense
of the penitent's responsibility to the whole Church in time and
space. God, Mary, the saints and the apostles are invoked as
witnesses to this act of contrition. There is a sense of complete-
ness about the list of those who are invoked: Mary, Gabriel and
Michael; St John the Baptist and then other apostles and those
who have proclaimed the faith in every age. The inclusion of
the first three ecumenical councils as the source for right
doctrine is interesting. Given that the Syriac Orthodox Church
recognizes the first seven councils as authoritative, perhaps this
gives us a clue as to the date of the composition of these prayers
or perhaps their inclusion in the liturgy of the Church.

Penance is normally dispensed in church with the priest
sitting in a chair. It is a sacrament for which the faithful prepare
carefully and which they will receive only occasionally. The
priest has the authority given by the Church to forgive sins in
Christ's name, and pronounces absolution always mindful of
his own sinfulness.

Syrian Prayers for the Kiss of Peace

Maundy Thursday

O Christ, our God, who by your mystical Supper have
brought to an end the old and symbolic service and
delivered to us the new mystery of grace, we beseech
you, O Lord, to make us partners and partakers of your
holy and mystical Supper; and make us worthy to enjoy
it in purity and without condemnation, that through it
we may be delivered from all the darkness of sin and be
well-pleasing to you by our inward and outward deeds
in this present life and in the eternal one; and make us
worthy, O Lord, to enjoy the sweet beatitudes of your
Kingdom and your heavenly feast.

On account of all your grace towards us we offer to
you glory, worship and thanksgiving, and to your Father
who sent you for our salvation, and to your all-holy,
good, adorable and life-giving Spirit, who is of one
substance with you now and for ever.

Holy Saturday

O Christ, our God, after having fulfilled your divine
dispensation in the flesh for our sake and suffering
passion and crucifixion, you descended into Sheol to
grant hope and consolation to the dead. You have
revealed this mystery in your person in order to purify
and absolve from the defilement of sin all those who
believe in you, and have promised them to enjoy it with
you anew in your Kingdom.

Make us worthy to be partners and partakers of this
mystical and heavenly delight, and grant us that in purity
and without condemnation we partake of it so that, by
partaking of it, we may be united with you in the true
and indivisible life and gain in you incorruptibility and

eternal felicity; and we offer up praise, honour and
thanksgiving to you, and to your Father, and to your
Holy Spirit, now, always and for ever.

These are two good examples of seasonal material being used
at the peace. On Maundy Thursday the Church celebrates the
institution of the Lord's Supper. On Holy Saturday, the Eastern
tradition has it that Christ preached to the souls in hell, thus
extending the possibility of salvation to the dead as well as the
living.

Syrian Prayers for the Morning

God help us.
The stormy winds and waves of sins that we committed
   are encircling us.
May you be the port of peace for us, that we may not
   sink in the sea of sins.
We are waiting to repent.
As you extended your hand to Peter, extend your hand
   to us and help us.

O Christ, our Lord,
you offered yourself as a pleasing incense before God the
   Father.
Because of you, we may be a pleasing incense before
   God.
Though our prayers and offerings are abominable and
   foul smelling,
touch and purify us with your holy hand which cleansed
   the lepers
to make our prayers and offerings sweet smelling
   fragrances.
Barekhmor [Bless my Lord].

For the intercession of Mother of God

God our Lord,
by your presence you shook Mount Zion.
While you were bearing the heights and the depths,
you willed that Virgin Mary conceive you without
   marriage
and bring you forth ineffably.
May your mother's name be glorified, and help us by her
   prayers.

For the intercession of saints

Martyrs! Pray for us,
that he may have mercy on us by his grace
and save us from the punishment of the last day.
Pray for us that we may be made worthy to see you
when you receive the victorious crowns.

For the intercession of the patron saint

St [Name], those who are in distress seek your help.
May your prayer be a fortress and refuge for us.
By your prayers, may our petitions be granted,
sick people be healed, and those who are being tempted
    by Satan be liberated.

Repentance

O God,
you do not deny your mercy to the sinners who call
    upon you.
By your compassion, spare us from punishments and the
    rods of wrath.
To praise you for your mercy, grant us joyful months
    and prosperous years.
By the glorious sign of your cross, guard us from the
    evil.
Lord, may we not be silent from praising you,
and withdrawn from glorifying you.
Lord, do not judge us according to your righteousness.
We confess that we are sinners.
If you judge us according to our sins, we cannot hope
    for eternal life
and cannot plead before you, and shall inherit the fires
    of hell.
Therefore, according to your mercy, pardon and forgive
    our sins.
Lord, when you judge us, let our sins not conceal us.

When the righteous are clothed in glory, may we not be
naked at the judgement.
We confess that we have fallen in sin;
extend your hand to us that we may stand again.
O compassionate One, who open the door to all those
who repent,
have mercy on us as you forgave the thief on the cross at
your side.

For the departed

Lord, grant peace and good memory to our departed
fathers and brothers.
Include them in the company of saints and in their ranks.
When you sit at the throne for judgement and to
separate the righteous from the evil, may they receive
your compassion.
When you appear in your grace, may they stand on your
right side.
O Lord, open your great door full of mercy.
Hear our petitions and show mercy to our souls.
O glorious light which enlightens all creation in the
morning,
enlighten our intellects so that we may praise your
mercy.

The prayer for the day may be said here.

Lord, it is good to give thanks to you
and to sing praise to your exalted name,
to proclaim your goodness in the morning
and your faithfulness in the night.
Lord, hear my voice in the morning.
May I be seen ready before you in the morning.
Lord, have compassion on your people.
Lord, pardon and forgive all our sins.
Holy One, let your right hand overshadow us
and your Name heal our weaknesses.

Each of these morning prayers in the Syrian tradition has as its kernel a scriptural incident or allusion. In the case of the first prayer, it is Jesus walking on the water and preventing Peter from sinking. We begin our prayer with something familiar to us before using it as a springboard for a hope or petition.

In the prayer of intercession for the Mother of God the typically Syrian device of paradox is used creatively. Christ is the Word, the Creator of the world and yet is conceived by Mary. In the sense the Creator is created. Syrian Christianity uses these paradoxes in order to try and convey, without diminishing, the majesty and complexity of the mystery of Christ's activity.

Syrian Prayers during Passiontide

Blessed it is that you humbled yourself for us.
Christ, by your Passion you saved us from our sins.
    Accept our offerings and have mercy on us. *(3 times)*
O Lord, let there be praise to you, and honour to your
    Father, and adoration and glory to the Holy Spirit.
O Lord, have mercy and compassion on us, sinners.
May the gates of the heavenly Jerusalem be opened,
that our prayers may enter into the throne of Christ.
O Lord, we praise you.
O Lord, we praise you.
O Lord, you are our hope, and we praise you for ever.
Our Father who art in heaven . . .

Thursday of the Great Passover

Blessed are you that humbled yourself for us.
Christ, who by your Passover replaced the paschal lamb,
    rejoice us with your Passover and have mercy on us.
O Lord, let there be praise to you and honour to your
    Father and adoration and glory to the Holy Spirit.
O Lord, have mercy and compassion on us, sinners.
May the gates of the heavenly Jerusalem be opened,
that our prayers may enter into the throne of Christ.
O Lord, we praise you.
O Lord, we praise you.
O Lord, you are our hope, and we praise you for ever,
Our Father who art in heaven . . .

Holy Week is a time when Christians feel particularly close to
the foundational events of their faith. At the beginning of Holy
Week we recall Christ entering Jerusalem, so it is unsurprising
that the prayer focuses on Christ and his relationship to the
heavenly Jerusalem. Neither is it surprising that in the prayer

for Maundy Thursday, the day when we recall the institution of the Eucharist in a Passover meal, our attention is drawn to Jesus, the Passover Lamb of God who presides over the meal itself. Mystery is handled with care and dignity.

Syrian Supplication to the Blessed Virgin

Celebrant O compassionate Lord, open to us the door of
your mercies and do not make us ashamed as we
have put our confidence in you. Deliver us and
save us from all distress and intolerable
temptations, as you are the Saviour and the
Redeemer of those who believe in you. Have
mercy upon us, O Lord, have mercy upon us,
because you are our trust and our hope. Do not be
angry with us for ever, and do not remember our
hidden and known offences and transgressions.
According to the abundance of your mercy,
compassion and loving kindness, save us from our
enemies, as you are our God, we are your people,
the creation of your hands, and we are called by
your holy Name. We ask these spiritual gifts by
virtue of the prayers and intercession of your
Mother the holy Virgin Mary. Have compassion
and mercy upon us, O Good One.

People Halleluiah, halleluiah, halleluiah.

The people shall sing the following hymn:

People O pride of the faithful,
offer petition on our behalf to the only-begotten
who sprang forth from you,
that he may have mercy upon us all.

Deacon The mystery which was hidden from generations
and ages was revealed to you, O Fount of
Chastity, when the Archangel Gabriel came and
greeted you, saying: 'Hail, O full of grace, the
Lord is with you, you are blessed among women'
[Luke 1.28].

Hail, O land that was never sown.
Hail, O bush that was set aflame, but was not
    consumed.
Hail, O depth which is hard for sight to fathom.
Hail, O bridge that leads to the height and the
    ladder that lifts up into heaven.
Hail, O vessel in which the divine manna was
    preserved.
Hail, O you who abolished the curse of old time.
Hail, O you who lifted up Adam from his fall.
The Lord is with you.
Kyrie eleison. Kyrie eleison. Kyrie eleison.

The people shall sing the following hymn:

People   O Christ, our Lord and Creator,
have mercy upon us by your Mother's intercession.
Set us free from the deception of the devil
and deliver us from his powers.
We are your servants and to you we commit
    ourselves, hoping for your mercies,
for we have no other Redeemer than you.
Pardon us and pardon our departed ones, and
    grant us full forgiveness.

This prayer of supplication begins by addressing God directly
but soon turns its attention to Mary. It is she with whom the
people of God intercede. But Mary always points beyond
herself to the incarnate Lord. The prayer then explores the
mystery of Mary's achievement. Characteristic of this tradition,
a rich mix of metaphor and paradoxical allusion combine to
create a spiritual 'space' in which the extent of the mystery is
acknowledged but never defined. Finally, the petitions move
back to address Christ directly.

The Blessing of an Icon in the Syrian Tradition

Glory be to the Father, to the Son, and to the Holy Spirit.

O Lord, God of the whole incorporeal and perceptible creation, the Maker of the heavenly hosts, earthly beings and all that is under the earth, you have filled your Church with the likeness of the firstborn who are written in your heavenly Church and who minister to you with your Holy Spirit. Grant, O Lord God, that your powerful and omnipotent right hand may protect, bless and sanctify this icon for the adoration of your most honoured Name. May all those who call upon you in true faith and ask of your compassion with a pure heart, receive their good requests, and present to you first-fruits and oblations so as to obtain health and healing and to attain the salvation of their souls. We beseech you and make supplication to you to accomplish your command and fulfil the promise of your most Holy Spirit so that the gospel precept may dwell, operate, perfect and diligently regard every deed or word that is done or said in the name of this icon. We ask this favour by your loving kindness, the mercies and love for mankind of your only-begotten Son, our Lord God and Saviour Jesus Christ, with whom you are rightly ascribed praise, honour and dominion, with your Holy Spirit, now, always and for ever.

Deacons   ✛ Amen.

Priest   O Lord our God, by the prayers of your Mother and of all your saints, martyrs, apostles and St [Name].

Here he anoints the icon with oil, not chrism, saying:

Priest   In the name of the Father ✛.

Deacons   ✛ Amen.

144

Priest	And of the Son ✠.
Deacons	✠ Amen.
Priest	And of the Holy Spirit ✠, for life eternal.
Deacons	Amen.

In many of the Eastern Christian Churches, icons are important for personal and public devotion. Within the Oriental Orthodox tradition icons are used perhaps in a slightly less formal way than in the Chalcedonian tradition, the emphasis being on depicting a story or event in the life of our Lord, Mary or another saint, rather than on the strictly formal vocabulary of classical iconography. But that means that icons in the Ethiopian, Coptic or Syrian styles often have an immediacy and vitality that classical icons lack. But then they are doing different things. Rather than being windows into the heart of the sacred, they are inciting and feeding different, but no less valid, sorts of prayer. An Oriental Orthodox icon points us more to a story and the people engaged in it than to abstract theological realities.

This prayer for the blessing of an icon begins with the praise and recognition of God the Creator of all that is in earth and in heaven. And it is in this context of creation that God is asked to place his benediction on the particular icon. The purpose, whatever the image, is praise of the Creator. The icon leads the worshipper to praise and worship of God: not of the image on the board; not of the saint who is depicted. All are windows, vehicles, a means to an end. The icon only has validity and authority in so far as it points towards God, the author of all.

There is liberation here, the liberation of imagination to use images and creativity to explore our faith not just in words, but in pictures, things that inspire us and feed the eyes and the heart.

The Society for Promoting Christian Knowledge (SPCK) was founded in 1698. Its mission statement is:

To promote Christian knowledge by
- **Communicating the Christian faith in its rich diversity;**
- **Helping people to understand the Christian faith and to develop their personal faith; and**
- **Equipping Christians for mission and ministry.**

SPCK Worldwide serves the Church through Christian literature and communication projects in over 100 countries, and provides books for those training for ministry in many parts of the developing world. This worldwide service depends upon the generosity of others and all gifts are spent wholly on ministry programmes, without deductions.

SPCK Bookshops support the life of the Christian community by making available a full range of Christian literature and other resources, providing support for those training for ministry, and assisting bookstalls and book agents throughout the UK.

SPCK Publishing produces Christian books and resources, covering a wide range of inspirational, pastoral, practical and academic subjects. Authors are drawn from many different Christian traditions, and publications aim to meet the needs of a wide variety of readers in the UK and throughout the world.

The Society does not necessarily endorse the individual views contained in its publications, but hopes they stimulate readers to think about and further develop their Christian faith.

For further information about the Society, visit our website at *www.spck.org.uk,* or write to:
SPCK, Holy Trinity Church, Marylebone Road,
London NW1 4DU, United Kingdom.